JB JOSSEY-BASS™
A Wiley Brand

T0319509

96 Ways to Make Your Website More Donor, Member & Volunteer Friendly

Scott C. Stevenson, Editor

WILEY

978-1-118-69252-3   ISBN

978-1-118-70425-7   ISBN (online)

96 Ways to Make Your Website More Donor, Member & Volunteer Friendly

Published by

Stevenson, Inc.

P.O. Box 4528 • Sioux City, Iowa • 51104

Phone 712.239.3010 • Fax 712.239.2166

www.stevensoninc.com

TABLE OF CONTENTS

Article Designation Key: Donors ▪▪▪▪ Members ▪▪▪▪ Volunteers ▪▪▪▪

TABLE OF CONTENTS

Article Designation Key: Donors ▬▬▬   Members ▬▬▬   Volunteers ▬▬▬

96 Ways to Make Your Website More Donor, Member & Volunteer Friendly

 ### 1 Publicize Your Members Through Your Website ▬ ▬ ▬

Seeking a creative, non-traditional benefit for your membership? Offer a link to member websites from your organization's website.

The Kansas Auctioneers Association, Inc. (KAA) of Newton, KS and the Citizens for the Arts in Pennsylvania (Harrisburg, PA) offer this benefit. It was a marketing decision for both.

LaDonna Schoen, executive director, KAA, says members have been taking advantage of this benefit for the past nine years. "The KAA's decision was a public relations move to better inform the public about the advantage of hiring professionals in our field."

One hundred fifteen members utilize the option. "The cross linking of the websites attracts a greater number of clients to our site. The more avenues to reach potential clients, the stronger the association becomes and the more our members benefit from the increased publicity," says Schoen.

Jenny Hershour, managing director, Citizens for the Arts in Pennsylvania, says "Member organizations should market members and that's why we have offered this feature on our website over the past 14 years. We thought our visitors should be able to click on our members' hyperlinks and go directly to their website."

Almost three-fourths of the organization's 300 members take advantage of the benefit.

To view KAA's website, visit: www.kansasauctioneers. com/members/sites.php. For the Citizens for the Arts in Pennsylvania, visit: www.paarts.org.

Source: LaDonna Schoen, Executive Director, Kansas Auctioneers Association, Inc., Newton, KS. Phone (316) 283-7780. E-mail: kaaauct@cox.net
Jenny L. Hershour, Managing Director, Citizens for the Arts in Pennsylvania, Harrisburg, PA. Phone (717) 234-0959. E-mail: jlh@paarts.org

 ### 2 Enhance Your Website to Reel in More Volunteers ▬ ▬ ▬

How effective is your organization's website at attracting volunteers? Does it account for 10, 30 or 50 percent of your new volunteer candidates?

What if you could say 100 percent?

That is being accomplished at Sydney Cooper Senior Smiles (Los Angeles, CA), a 100-percent volunteer-run nonprofit that provides companionship to the elderly.

"Potential volunteers see we're creative, that we take a different approach to volunteering," says Jill Pizitz-Hochstein, executive director.

The organization's website (www.seniorsmiles.org) is interactive and draws surfers in with a cartoon illustrating the need for volunteers, she says. The site gives multiple options to start volunteering by simply clicking a mouse.

Pizitz-Hochstein told webmaster and volunteer Andrew Zaw she wanted the website to be fun, interesting and interactive. Zaw put in a lot of hours to make that happen. He created the website for free, but Senior Smiles does pay for the domain and name.

Zaw spends two to six hours a week maintaining the site.

Potential volunteers are drawn to the website by posts on Volunteermatch.org, Craigslist.org, through trainings and flyers. Pizitz-Hochstein emphasizes that it's important to make volunteering as easy as possible.

Senior Smiles has hundreds of seniors waiting for a companion, which emphasizes the importance of making the volunteering experience enjoyable, notes Catherine Kim, volunteer coordinator.

"We believe an organization like ours should be easy to join so potential volunteers can begin their volunteer experience when they are interested," Kim says. "I realized from my

personal experiences with other volunteer organizations that the longer an organization takes to contact and/or begin the volunteer, the more the potential volunteer loses interest."

Sources: Jill Pizitz-Hochstein, Executive Director, and Catherine Kim, Volunteer Coordinator, Sydney Cooper Senior Smiles, Los Angeles, CA. Phone (310) 459-0490. E-mail: seniorsmiles4u@seniorsmiles.org

3 Showcase Naming Gift Opportunities Online

Looking for more ways to market naming gift opportunities? Why not make them available on your website?

Officials with Children's Healthcare of Atlanta (Atlanta, GA) not only provide naming gift opportunities on their website, they allow visitors to categorize those opportunities by specialty or price range.

Although visitors cannot reserve or contribute to naming opportunities on the website, they can explore naming opportunities that interest them. It's basically just for shopping, says Jane Ellington, director of donor relations.

For more information, visit: www.choa.org/ campaign/NamingOpps/index.asp

Source: Jane Ellington, Director of Donor Relations, Children's Healthcare of Atlanta, Atlanta, GA. Phone (404) 785-7336. E-mail: jane.ellington@choa.org

4   Internet Offers Innovative Ways to Communicate, Recruit ▪ ▪ ▪

The Internet offers numerous opportunities to foster volunteer relationships.

As an easy, inexpensive, quick way to get the word out about last-minute or current volunteer needs in the community, the Jewish Federation of Metropolitan Chicago's TOV Volunteer Network (Chicago, IL) creates a monthly hotsheet of volunteer opportunities. The document is created in Microsoft Publisher, turned into a PDF file using Adobe Acrobat and posted on the organization's website. It is also mailed as a link and in plain text format to a mass e-mail list of 2,400 people. Hard copies are distributed to staff and various community members to hand out to interested parties.

Each hotsheet features six to 15 volunteer opportunities. Most people respond via e-mail, although some phone, says Tracy Klevens More, director of volunteer services.

The hotsheet's e-mail list is made up of anyone who has done volunteer work for the organization over the past several years, or has expressed interest in volunteering, says More. They range in age from teens to the elderly. People are removed from the list only at their request.

Any organization can contact Jewish Federation and ask them to recruit volunteers for their projects. Those that make the hotsheet are usually last-minute, current needs in the community, but can also be jobs that require unique skills.

Source: Tracy Klevens More, Director, Volunteer Services, Jewish Federation of Metropolitan Chicago, Chicago, IL. Phone (312) 444-2810. E-mail: tracymore@juf.org

5   Offer Members The Option to Update Online ▪ ▪ ▪

For the Institute of Electrical and Electronics Engineers, Inc. (IEEE) of Piscataway, NJ, the benefits of allowing members to update their contact information online far outweighs any disadvantages.

Since eliminating the middle man in 1998, Cecelia Jankowski, managing director, regional activities, says members and IEEE have reaped the benefits of the online option.

Jankowski says by allowing members to update their contact information online it creates flexibility for the members, reduces complaints about inaccurate member records and saves time administratively.

Now instead of staff focusing efforts on reentering data, they can address issues that were placed on the back burner, such as member outreach and development programs.

IEEE's update profile application also enables members to change technical interest areas, mailing list preferences and credit card information.

Jankowski says that of IEEE's 370,000 members, roughly one-third of members change something in their records annually and 30,000 members access the update profile application monthly.

"I encourage any member organization to at least explore the option because anyone working with members is going to want to be able to have the most current data on hand," she says.

Before rushing into a decision, Jankowski says, organizations should consider cost; their organization's size; how frequently they contact their members; products and services offered; how the service will be implemented; and security and privacy issues.

Source: Cecelia Jankowski, Managing Director, Regional Activities, IEEE, Piscataway, NJ. Phone (732) 562-5504. E-mail: c.jankowski@ieee.org

6   Solicit Major Gifts Through Your Website ▪

To spur online giving, Carnegie Mellon University (Pittsburgh, PA) launched an online giving site in conjunction with its $1 billion Inspire Innovation Campaign in October 2008.

Jay Brown, director of marketing, Web communications, says online giving has gone up 3 percent since they tied the website to the campaign.

In fiscal year 2008, Brown says, the university received an average of 245 gifts a month, with total monthly giving averaging $58,261. Most donors were alumni, with 26 percent of online donors directing their gift to the unrestricted Carnegie Mellon Fund.

The university's simplified, user-friendly online giving form (www.cmu.edu/campaign/ways/online.html) consists of three steps: About You, Your Gift and Payment. After completing each section, the donor clicks "Next" to move to the next page. Buttons throughout the university's website show users where they should click to give.

"We also keep looking for opportunities to drive more traffic to the site," Brown says, "such as advertising our online giving option in our quarterly magazine and adding a short link in every direct mail piece that connects people to the online form."

Online donors receive an automatically generated receipt and receive phone solicitations and other stewardship based on their giving level.

Source: Jay Brown, Director of Marketing for Web Communications, Carnegie Mellon University, Pittsburgh, PA. Phone (412) 268-1913. E-mail: jsbrown@andrew.cmu.edu

Article Designation Key:	Donors ▪▪▪▪	Members ▪▪▪▪	Volunteers ▪▪▪▪

7 Create a User-friendly Site ▪ ▪ ▪

Although a website generally won't, by itself, generate major gifts, it can help set the stage for such gifts.

The Web can get information about your mission broadly disseminated at a lower cost. Your site can help constituents better understand your programs and it's a great way to steward donors by letting them know how their gifts are being used.

"Your website should connect people to your organization, encourage support, increase your organization's awareness and entice others to care about your mission and programs," says Michel Hudson, owner, 501 Consulting (Round Rock, TX).

Hudson offers the following tips:

- Websites aren't just online brochures — they need to be dynamic and fresh so people return to learn new information.

- Writing for the Web requires an understanding of what does and doesn't work for online users. You may need to hire someone from outside your organization for this job.

- Use flash, videos and audio sparingly. People go to websites to find information, not to be dazzled by special effects. Your constituents may not have high-speed access and you don't want to lose them while they're waiting for pictures to appear.

- Keep navigation simple and logical. Offer downloads of useful forms and articles, especially those relating to donations, campaigns and programs. Use easy-to-read graphics, colors and fonts (e.g., Arial or Verdana). Different monitors and browsers interpret Web pages differently, so be sure to test your site in various ways.

- Offer easy, secure donation methods.

"While most organizations won't be switching to a totally online fundraising program anytime soon," says Hudson, "the role the Internet plays in the lives of most donors makes it necessary for nonprofits to tap into that aspect of communication."

Source: Michel Hudson, CFRE, Owner, 501 Consulting, Round Rock, TX. Phone (512) 565-0142. E-mail: mhudson@501consulting.com

8 Virtual Reunions Keep Members Connected ▪

In an age where everyone is mobile, capturing members virtually seems like a logical step. Virtual reunions give members the ability to re-connect online, while keeping their information updated for the organization.

"Virtual reunions are indicative of the time we're in now. This couldn't be done 10 years ago when e-mail was just picking up," says Jon Allison, alumni and communications director, Salesianum School (Wilmington, DE).

The school has a dedicated Web page for virtual reunions that allows alumni to click on their school year. Each year brings up a page complete with found alumni and their contact information, alumni the school is looking for, plus reunion updates and class news.

Each page also has a spot for alumni to input their own information, which Allison uses to update the database. While the virtual reunion page goes back to the graduation class of 1942, Allison says that younger members, at least five years out of school, are most likely to take advantage of the system — which is wonderful, since this age group is more likely to move around in the years following graduation.

Andrew Christopherson, director, alumni programs, Carolina Alumni Association (Columbia, SC), says a virtual system makes it easier to keep track of members and offers alumni who have moved away the chance to re-connect with classmates.

The Carolina Alumni Association offers its members an online professional and social network called the Gamecock Network. There are 240,000 online members and once a profile is created, it's automatically downloaded into the organization's system.

Both Allison and Christopherson say they continually draw members to the virtual reunion pages by marketing the site in other alumni material, including newsletters, magazines, links from the organization's other Web pages and e-mails.

Sources: Jon Allison, Alumni & Communications Director, Salesianum School, Wilmington, DE. Phone (302) 654-2495, ext. 143. E-mail: jallison@salesianum.org Andrew Christopherson, Director of Alumni Programs, Carolina Alumni Association, University of South Carolina, Columbia, SC. Phone (803) 777-3473. E-mail: christoa@gwm.sc.edu

9   Drive Members to Website With a Scavenger Hunt ■ ■ ■

Lure members to your organization's website with an online scavenger hunt.

Marketing staff with the Cable & Telecommunications Association for Marketing (CTAM) of Alexandria, VA developed a scavenger hunt to drive traffic to their website while also highlighting exclusive member resources, says Shelly Good-Cook, senior director of membership marketing and chapter relations.

The goal was to enhance the perceived value of membership and to reinforce membership renewal, says Good-Cook.

They developed the contest through a series of eight postcards sent by the postal service two business days apart, with matching e-mails timed to appear on the same day as the mailed piece.

The first postcard was a teaser that didn't identify CTAM.

The next postcard revealed the organization, told the members a contest was coming and suggested they could win a high-definition TV.

The next four cards contained five pertinent questions and instructions on conference participation.

The final postcard recapped questions and instructions.

"It was an enjoyable, high-energy campaign," says Good-Cook. "Members had to dig to find the right answers on a number of questions. Certain website content wasn't accessed frequently before the contest. Therefore, increased traffic to those pages was a direct result of the contest.

"About two percent of our membership entered all of the correct answers."

For legal reasons, she notes, be sure to provide a way for nonmembers to participate in your online scavenger hunt or contest. In this case, CTAM allowed nonmembers to e-mail requests to be entered into the drawing for prizes. Nonmembers, however, were not allowed to search for answers on the website.

Source: Shelly Good-Cook, Senior Director of Membership Marketing & Chapter Relations, Cable & Telecommunications Association for Marketing, Alexandria, VA. Phone (703) 549-4200. E-mail: shelly@ctam.com

10   Five Ways to Attract Volunteers Via Your Website ■ ■ ■

Many volunteer-reliant organizations find that online recruitment is a great way of finding new people.

Wendy Bojin-Liston, manager of volunteer services, Special Olympics of Northern California (Pleasant Hill, CA), uses these steps to turn online inquiries into volunteers:

1. **Ensure site is easy to find.** Have your IT department review your website's metadata section for key words that will ensure your site will pop up during various Web searches. In addition, partner with volunteer organizations that exist to place volunteers where they are needed by creating links between your website and theirs.

2. **Make registration easy.** Keep the application short. Bojin-Liston advises, "Find out a little bit about the volunteer's interest so you can have the appropriate staff member follow up with them to get additional information."

3. **Respond to inquiries quickly.** The worst move an organization can make is to put time and money into online registration but neglect to establish its system for timely follow up. Waiting too long to contact potential volunteers could mean losing the volunteer to another organization.

4. **Give multiple options.** If possible, let volunteers choose between specific events or volunteering on an ongoing basis. Some volunteers may be dynamite but not able to make a long-term commitment. Also, supply job descriptions online so potential volunteers know the expectations of each opportunity and can better select those that fit.

5. **Be willing to make changes to your website.** When Special Olympics of Northern California couldn't find information on volunteers who had applied online, Bojin-Liston says they took action. "We fine-tuned our process to make it easier for volunteers and worked with our IT department to ensure applications were flagged for immediate attention." Bojin-Liston says volunteer feedback regarding the application process and a good relationship with the IT department are keys to success in online recruitment.

Source: Wendy Bojin-Liston, Manager of Volunteer Services, Special Olympics of Northern California, Pleasant Hill, CA. Phone (925) 944-8801. E-mail: wbliston@sonc.org

---

Key Metadata Search Words

To ensure your website appears in Web search results, include these keywords in the metadata section of your website:

- Volunteer opportunities
- Volunteering
- Helping people
- Event
- Entertainment
- Youth, families, kids and/or environment

---

11 Advice for Creating User-friendly Online Wish List ■ ■ ■

Could your organization benefit from an online wish list?

Officials with the Mountain View Branch, Anchorage Public Library (Anchorage, AK), realized such a project could offer a unique opportunity to help fill new bookshelves added in the branch's expansion project.

Linda Klein, youth services librarian, says since launching the wish list in November 2007, some 80 items have been purchased for the youth literature section.

"Donors responded to the wish list project immediately," says Klein. "During a fundraising event for the branch, we set up a laptop and unveiled the Amazon wish list page (www.amazon.com/gp/registry/wishlist/K73U9TAJQ707/ref=cm_wl_rlist_go). We had a few donors make purchases that very night."

Klein answers a few questions about the wish list program:

"What is an online wish list program?"

"Much like a bridal registry, online wish lists allow you to identify a specific set of items that your organization needs. The needed items are posted on the seller's website as a wish list allowing donors to purchase the specified items from the list. The items are then sent directly to the organization from the seller."

"Why did your organization decide to implement such a program?"

"This wish list project was created to benefit one of our library branches that was closed in May 2007 and will soon be reopened. Because the branch will be greatly expanded when reopened, and its collection is in need of many new materials, we decided to use an online program to make it easy for people to support the library in a concrete way."

"How does the program work?"

"We set up a nonprofit account with Amazon (www.amazon.com) that is accessed with a user name and password so we can control the content of the wish list. The program allows us to place a description about the wish list and how it would serve our library on the Amazon site.

"I had compiled a list of books, primarily children's and young adult literature, since that is the area with the greatest need because of the expansion at the library branch. I searched through Amazon's site for the titles, and with little more than a click of a button I added them to the wish list. As items were purchased, I replenished the wish list with different titles from my original list.

"For library patrons, it's easy to make a gift. They can find a link to the Amazon wish list from our Web page. From there, they can see the items we've identified, how much it costs, and whether or not it has been purchased by someone else."

"How do you recognize the donors who make purchases from the wish list?"

"We place a label inside each book explaining that the item was purchased through the generous support of our wish list by library patrons."

"How does the library promote the wish list?"

"There is a link on our website which goes to a page that explains the functions of the wish list. That page has a link directly to the Amazon wish list. We have also promoted the program using bookmarks and through a link on the branch's Web page."

"What advice would you offer other nonprofits interested in creating an online wish list?"

"Go with a reputable company that has experience with online wish lists. Amazon has been used by other libraries for this kind of function, so we felt confident that we could benefit from their experience. Identify a specific need or target group you are trying to benefit rather than scattershot trying to solve all your problems with a wish list. It is easier to manage and promote a list that has a specific focus."

Source: Linda Klein, Youth Services Librarian, Muldoon Branch, Anchorage Public Library, Anchorage, AK. Phone (907) 343-4032. E-mail: kleinlm@muni.org

Steps to Create Your Online Wish List

If your organization is interested in pursuing an online wish list program, Linda Klein, youth services librarian, Anchorage Public Library (Anchorage, AK), recommends these steps:

1. **Identify the need you are trying to fill.** "We knew from studying the neighborhood that this library would serve a large immigrant population and many families with small children," says Klein. The branch was also aware of its gap in the collection.

2. **Develop a master list.** To populate the wish list, Klein created a master list of every book she thought the library should have for the juvenile and young adult sections. "I used resources such as award-winner lists, websites with recommended books and publications (books and magazines) to identify the 'must-haves' for any juvenile collection," she says.

3. **Involve interested parties in your wish list.** "Decide who in your organization will have access to the account and share the login information with those people," she says. "We formed a small impromptu committee of our collection development specialist and our technical services librarian and others to iron out the details (e.g., what materials to include or not, whether to acknowledge individual donors, and how to word the blurb on Amazon's site and our website)."

4. **Set up your account.**

5. **Populate the wish list.** By using your master list and matching your needs with what is available at the bookseller's site, create your online wish list. Keep track on your master list what has been added to the list, items purchased and new titles for purchase.

12 Display a Virtual Donor Wall on Your Website ▪ ▪ ▪

You may have a donor wall in your lobby that depicts the names of past donors, or perhaps you have a walkway with named bricks displaying the names of donors. Why not use that same approach and create a visually appealing virtual wall on your website?

Whether it's a donor wall or a giving tree that lists donors, come up with a creative way of displaying names of donors on your website. It's yet another way to give donors the recognition they deserve; it can be easily viewed by donors whose geographic distance prevents them from visiting your facility or campus.

Examples of Virtual Donor Walls

www.alsa.org (Amyotrophic Lateral Sclerosis Association, Calabasas Hills, CA) Click on "Donate," then scroll down and click on "Virtual Donor Wall."

www.seattlecenter.org (Seattle Center Fund, Seattle, WA) Click "How to Give," then click on "Virtual Donor Wall."

www.dentalmuseum.org (National Museum of Dentistry, Baltimore, MD) Click on "Get Involved," then go to "Annual Fund Contributors."

13 Offer Quick Answers With Q&A Web Page ▪ ▪ ▪

Staff with the Houston Zoo (Houston, TX) save time and resources by posting answers to members' and others' frequently asked questions online.

Some of the 35 questions and answers on the zoo website's Q&A section include:

Q: *When will I get my membership card?*
A: Your membership card should arrive within two to three weeks from time of purchase. If you mail your payment in, please allow additional time for processing.

Q: *May I visit before I get my card?*
A: Sure! Just bring your photo ID and your membership receipt, or a printed copy of the e-mail confirmation if you purchased online, and stop by the membership window to verify your purchase and receive your free entry to the zoo.

Q: *When does my membership expire?*
A: Your membership will expire one year from the date of purchase.

The goal in designing the member Q&A page was simple: "One-stop 'answer hopping,'" says Elizabeth Garza, director of membership. "We wanted the page to be a resource not just for Web visitors considering a first-time zoo membership purchase, but for current members as well. We review the Q&A section regularly to keep the information fresh and up to date."

Benefits of adding such a Web page include minimizing redundant questions received by phone and e-mail, Garza says. In addition, members will appreciate the ease and convenience of finding this information readily available online.

Source: Elizabeth Garza, Director of Membership, Houston Zoo, Houston, TX. E-mail: egarza@houstonzoo.org

14 Conduct an Online Donor Survey ▪ ▪ ▪

Use the growing possibilities of the Internet to maximize your fundraising capabilities.

St. Jude Children's Research Hospital (Memphis, TN) recently added an online donor survey to its website to help improve interactions with supporters, says Sandra Sellers, donor services representative. The survey asks:

• "Are you a current donor?"

• "How likely are you to make a donation in the next 12 months?"

• "How could St. Jude improve your overall satisfaction?"

At the end of the survey, respondents have the option to add contact information.

Sellers says their website reaches some donors they may not normally reach through regular mail. It is also another avenue to reach more donors.

"I call or e-mail all donors who fill out the survey and share my specific contact information with them so that they can direct any further comments or questions directly to me," says Sellers. "If the information deals with another department, I would share the information with them."

She says they receive three to 10 responses weekly, noting that the website is a new feature that they're not currently promoting: "We're curious as to who will find it on their own and how many will respond to it without any prompting to do so."

To view St. Jude's online donor survey, go to www.stjude.org and click on "Ways to Help" in the upper right-hand corner, then go to the "Making a Difference" section on the bottom right and click on "Tell us about your donor experience."

Source: Sandra Sellers, Donor Services Representative, St. Jude Children's Research Hospital, Memphis, TN. Phone (800) 805-5856. E-mail: Sandra.sellers@stjude.org

Article Designation Key: Donors ▬▬▬   Members ▬▬▬   Volunteers ▬▬▬

15   How Blogging Fits Into the Volunteer Experience ▬ ▬ ▬

Are your volunteers scattered throughout the region or country? Is their interaction limited to special events and occasional meetings? Are you looking for a way to bring them together without spending a lot of money?

Earlier this year, Project Linus NJ, Inc. (Keyport, NJ), a nonprofit organization that creates handmade blankets, preemie sets and toys for children suffering serious illness and trauma, opened a private Web log or blog for its volunteers.

The organization's president, Hillary Roberts, came up with the idea after reading about blog journaling in Wired magazine and asking her volunteers if they would be interested in starting one. Since many volunteers never meet face to face — they are scattered throughout New Jersey and surrounding states — Roberts thought a blog would be the ideal way to build solidarity. Members responded with a resounding "yes" and quickly named the blog site "Comfort Station."

A virtual volunteer (a college student) offered 20 hours of community service to set up the blog. The organization used a blog engine, similar to a Web search engine, to recruit the student.

Comfort Station offers volunteers the opportunity to share personal stories, humor and uplifting messages privately with one another. Roberts takes time every week to read the entries.

"I've learned a great deal about our volunteers through their blogs — why they offer their time and talents and how mutual the experience has been for many," she says. "Much of their own healing and volunteer spirit is expressed through their blogs."

In less than a year, about 900 volunteers participated in blogging, with nearly 3,000 posts. Roberts says the posts give a pulse to the enthusiasm of members; provide great random ideas for events newsletters and blanket patterns; and resolve many communication challenges.

As with personal journals or diaries, blogging is usually a private encounter. When creating a blog page for your volunteers, Roberts recommends keeping it private. Although blog pages can be used for other purposes (e.g., fundraising, recruiting, etc.), access should be restricted to group members only.

For more information on blogging, check out: www.blogging.com and www.blogger.com.

Source: Hillary Roberts, President, Project Linus NJ, Inc., Keyport, NJ. Phone (732) 335-9033. Email: BlankieDepo@aol.com. Website: www.blankiedepo.org

16   Social Networking Strengthens Member Community ▬ ▬ ▬

Social networking expands your organization's reach and invigorates your membership.

"With 14,000 members throughout the U.S. and around the world, we're constantly looking for ways to help members connect with one another and build community," says Jessica Medaille, senior director of membership development, International Society for Technology in Education (ISTE) in Eugene, OR. "We decided to try tapping into the popular social networking sites where so many students, young professionals and others connect. We developed a presence for ISTE on MySpace, FaceBook, LinkedIn and Second Life."

Social networking sites like the ones mentioned are not only useful for your current members but can also attract new members by exposing your organization to an entirely new community.

"We began developing our presence in these areas at the end of 2006. We now have 127 MySpace friends, 12 people have joined our FaceBook group and we recently started a LinkedIn group," says Medaille. "We've seen our biggest success with our Second Life presence. Second Life is a popular and fast-growing MUVE (Multi-user Virtual Environment) community. From December 2006 to the end of April nearly 1,100 people have joined our ISTE Second Life group. Some of these are also RL (real life) ISTE members and some have become ISTE members as a result."

Jennifer Ragan-Fore, director, general membership program, says most of the social networking sites they're using (MySpace, Facebook, LinkedIn) are completely free.

"These tools are great democratizers — even the smallest nonprofit can take advantage of these channels, often with even greater results than larger organizations, as smaller nonprofits are typically experienced in taking advantage of viral campaigns and their grassroots base."

Consider reaching out to your members to discover which social networking tools they are already using. Then find out which tools they'd be interested in using in the future. If you do decide to explore social networking options, make sure your members are aware of the sites you are using and how they can become involved.

"It's important to tailor the choice based on what will work for your group," says Ragan-Fore. "We have a special Web page devoted to this and have begun including it in our membership messaging and collateral. We include it in our member welcome e-mail and we plan to begin referencing it in printed materials."

Source: Jessica Medaille, Senior Director of Membership Development, International Society for Technology in Education (ISTE), Eugene, OR.
Jennifer Ragan-Fore, Director, General Membership Program, International Society for Technology in Education (ISTE), Eugene, OR.

Article Designation Key: Donors ▬▬▬   Members ▬▬▬   Volunteers ▬▬▬

17 Show Donors the Money (and Where It Goes) ▪ ▪ ▪

Anything you can do to show donors how their gifts make a difference will increase donors' confidence and make them more likely to give in the future.

Colleen Townsley Brinkmann, chief marketing officer, North Texas Food Bank (Dallas, TX), says a website illustration helps show donors where their food and financial donations go.

Visitors to the organization's website (www.ntfb.org) simply click on "Donate," then "Food" to find the link to the graphic chart, "Follow Your Donation."

Shown below, the graphic illustrates how food donations

Website Offers Giving Tools

Visitors to the North Texas Food Bank (Dallas, TX) website find several tools to encourage gifts. For example, starting at the home page (www.ntfb.org), visitors can:

Learn how to start an actual or virtual canned food drive — Click "Donate," "Food," and select "Conduct a Canned or Virtual Food Drive" in pop-up menu to register and receive tips for gathering food or cash gifts.

See inside the food bank — Select "About Us" and "Virtual Tour."

Share the passion — Click "Media Room" and "Video Features" for online videos explaining food bank programs and how they combat hunger in North Texas.

benefit 917 feeding and education programs in a 13-county area.

The page also helps educate donors and others about the work of the food pantry, which Townsley Brinkmann says is paramount: "We were having trouble getting people to understand we're not a cozy, little food pantry — we're a distribution agency. (And) by helping us you are helping tens of thousands of people."

The page averages 754 hits monthly.

Source: Colleen Townsley Brinkmann, Chief Marketing Officer; Mark Armstrong, Senior Manager-Internet and New Media, North Texas Food Bank, Dallas, TX. Phone (214) 347-9594.

Content not available in this edition

This online illustration shows North Texas Food Bank donors how their gifts help others.

18 Going Paperless Makes Teen Orientation Run Smoother ■ ■

Think about how much paper your volunteer office uses for each volunteer: application forms, volunteer handbooks, guidelines, orientation materials, etc. Now think about how much of that information could be put online.

That's exactly what Jamine Hamner, coordinator of volunteer services, Saint Joseph Health Care (Lexington, KY) did. A year ago Hamner and her staff wanted to streamline the teen volunteer program from a two-day orientation to a two-hour orientation.

What they did was create a paperless office with an online application system that works for the entire volunteer program.

A volunteer can search the available opportunities, complete and submit the application directly online. The applicant then receives an e-mail with instructions to complete the orientation online. The orientation materials — a confidentiality agreement, multiple choice safety test, multiple choice HIPAA test, volunteer agreement and orientation checklist — are all completed online and signed by the volunteer through electronic signature. As the applicant submits each item, it goes to Hamner's e-mail. She calls the volunteer and sets up an interview. During the interview she gets the required background information and finishes up the orientation process. Once the volunteer begins placement, each has their own login and password to check schedules and updates.

One of the biggest advantages to going paperless is the lack of wait time a volunteer has between applying and starting. Before going paperless, Hamner says, the application process took about one month, depending on if the volunteer signed up right after the monthly orientation. Now the process takes a week.

Hamner admits the office isn't entirely paperless. They do mail paper copies of forms to volunteers when needed — about one every three months. Hamner still requires one ink-to-paper signature for

the parental consent form for the teen volunteer program, which is accesible from the website.

Source: Jamine Hamner, Coordinator of Volunteer Services, Saint Joseph Health Care, Lexington, KY. Phone (859) 313-1290. E-mail: hamnerja@sjhlex.org

Advice for Setting Up A Paperless Office

Jamine Hamner, coordinator of volunteer services, Saint Joseph Health Care (Lexington, KY) says her office went paperless through trial and error. Now, that she's done it, Hamner says she'd never go back.

Hamner offers a list of essentials an organization must have when converting to a paperless office:

- Internet connection from your work computer.

- A website that allow you to upload documents.

- Your documents in an electronic format (e.g., Microsoft Word or PDF) that will be accessible.

- An online volunteer application that can be submitted from the website.

- Orientation forms, agreements, tests which can be created through your website.

- A separate place to store your electronic volunteer files, such as your organization's server or online file storage.

- A scanner with an automatic document feeder.

Hamner says before pursuing a paperless office it's important to ask your IT department if your website can support the transition. If not, Hamner says, by using a search engine organizations should be able to locate free and inexpensive options to create their own paperless office.

19 Use Your Website to Help Forge Alliances ■ ■ ■

"I'll scratch your back; you scratch mine."

Why not use your website to help forge relationships with others (businesses, associations, individuals) that can be mutually beneficial? To help make that happen:

✓ Offer brief profiles or features on particular organizations that you can rotate on a weekly or monthly basis.

✓ Include links to others' websites.

✓ List all existing partnerships followed by a brief description of each.

Others relish unsolicited publicity that puts them in a positive light. Why not use your website to help make that happen?

20 Offer Cost-effective, Accessible Membership Kits Online ▪

The Ottawa Valley Tourist Association (OVTA) of Pembroke, Ontario, Canada, offers a simple and cost-effective approach toward membership kits. Instead of mailing expensive hard copies of kits and incurring rising postage and printing costs, this membership organization offers a downloadable membership kit at its website.

The OVTA has more than 225 members, and officials continue to build on that with the accessible membership kit, which averages 97 downloads each month.

The kit consists of three PDFs: a membership benefits form (at right), as well as a membership application and advertising rate card.

The kit also alerts the OVTA to new businesses coming to the region and those in the planning stages, says Nicole Wilson, communications coordinator.

"It has become an extremely popular way to attract members," Wilson says. "With less paper and postage, it saves money while helping the environment. We are also looking into incorporating more interactive features through our new website that will be launched in the spring of 2009."

View the membership kit at www.ottawavalley.org.

Source: Nicole Wilson, Communications Coordinator, Ottawa Valley Tourist Association, Pembroke, Ontario, Canada. Phone (800) 757-6580.
E-mail: NWilson@countyofrenfrew.on.ca

Content not available in this edition

21 Use Your Website to Help Cultivate Major Gifts ▪ ▪ ▪

Although your website itself may not generate major gifts, what's on it can help nurture those gifts.

Here are examples of what may cultivate financially capable prospects who visit your website:

- Defining naming gift opportunities and listing them.
- Listing and describing existing named endowment funds.
- Doing feature articles on realized planned gifts and the donors.
- Touting your nonprofit's most significant achievements.
- Presenting facts, figures and history of your endowment.
- Displaying your board members' names and positions.
- Delineating planned gift opportunities.

- Sharing facts and figures that speak to your organization's fiscal strength.
- Citing the impact of past major gifts on your nonprofit and those you serve.
- Sharing information and updates regarding your capital campaign and/or strategic plan.
- Visibly sharing contact information of advancement personnel.
- Placing your case statement online.
- Describing the benefits of upper-end gift clubs and inviting participation.
- Including donor recognition measures.

Article Designation Key: Donors � Members ▬▬▬ Volunteers ▬▬▬

22 Online Recruitment Tip: Who Is info@yourwebsite.com? ■ ■ ■

Millions of people use the Internet every day and some of them are coming to your website for information on donating, becoming a member or volunteering. Don't run the risk of turning them away by not including your contact information on your site.

Avoid using a generic contact, such as info@ yourwebsite.com. Instead, list the name, phone number and e-mail address of the appropriate person for those departments within your organization that people can call or e-mail directly. In today's fast-paced, Internet world, impersonal contact contributes to the decline of good customer service — don't let it do so in your organization.

23 E-mail, Website Encourage New Chapter Development ■

How does your alumni association promote its alumni chapters and encourage new chapter development?

Officials with San Diego State University Alumni Association (San Diego, CA) offer constituents a user-friendly website that talks them through how to start or participate in a chapter and serve in a leadership role. The website divides chapters into four classifications: cultural/heritage, professional, shared interest and regional.

"With this day and age people are used to getting their information from the Web," says Diane Barragan, chapter coordinator. "We wanted to market the chapters not only on the Web but via e-mail and direct mail to provide our alums with greater awareness and visibility of chapters and chapter development."

The e-mail and website work hand-in-hand to successfully promote the association's alumni chapters.

"We send an alumni e-newsletter monthly that contains articles, event information and chapter updates," she says. "Every time a person clicks on the information, he or she is directed back to our website."

They promote the Web page at chapter events, driving people back to the Web page to register, find out more information and view event photo albums.

Since the alumni chapter's Web page went online five years ago, 23 chapters have been activated with more than 1,000 members worldwide.

Source: Diane Barragan, Chapter Coordinator, San Diego State University Alumni Association, San Diego, CA. Phone (619) 594-0947. E-mail: dbarraga@mail.sdsu.edu

Content not available in this edition

This Web page from the San Diego State University Alumni Association is designed to be highly user-friendly to the members in chapters throughout the world.

24   Website Showcases Volunteers of the Month ▬ ▬ ▬

Almost every volunteer-driven organization has some sort of recognition program. So what sets yours apart from others?

For the Humane Society of Williamson County (Leander, TX), volunteers are thanked for their contributions on a truly worldwide scale — through the humane society's website.

What originated as a volunteer of the quarter program became a monthly recognition when Memi Cardenas signed on as volunteer coordinator for the humane society.

"My decision to change the program was based on the fact that we have so many volunteers who do such great jobs that I would much rather recognize 12 than three," says Cardenas. "I think the more I can recognize and give back to them, the more we will create a stronger team."

Each month, Cardenas looks back over the previous month, gathering feedback from staff on who has excelled, made a difference or who has been volunteering for a long time but hasn't been acknowledged.

"The volunteer of the month can be someone who takes on a lot of responsibility as a team leader or someone who does something as simple but appreciated as walking the dogs a few times a week," says Cardenas.

The online profiles feature a photo and a biography highlighting the volunteer, what he/she has done for the organization and how long he/she has been volunteering.

Cardenas says the program is a great morale booster for her volunteers. "I have volunteers come up and ask me how they can become the volunteer of the month. It is a great motivator to get the other volunteers to try and achieve that acknowledgement."

Source: Memi Cardenas, Volunteer Coordinator, Humane Society of Williamson County, Leander, TX. Phone (512) 260-3602, ext. 106. E-mail: mcardenas@hswc.net

Volunteer of the Month features on the Humane Society of Williamson County website include photos, biographies and reasons why volunteers are being honored:

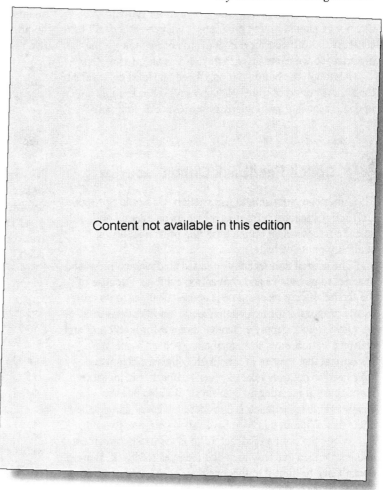

Content not available in this edition

25   Use Your Website to Get Sponsor Information Out ▬ ▬ ▬

"How do you use your website to share information with sponsors?"

"We have a page (www.louisvillezoo.org/support/sponsor/index.htm) designated for sponsorship information. This page includes prior sponsors, sponsorship benefits, sponsorship opportunities, a list of upcoming programs and events, and reasons for partnering with the zoo.

"We also have a page for potential sponsors requesting information on our largest fundraiser, The World's Largest Halloween Party (www.louisvillezoo.org/halloween). This site allows potential sponsors to familiarize themselves with the event before we meet with them. It contains significant demographic information, along with sponsor benefits including value of tangible and intangible assets based on valuation criteria provided by IEG, an industry leader in sponsorship/partnership marketing evaluation.

"Sometimes, depending on the level of sponsorship or the sponsor's needs, we can create an active link to their website from ours, driving customers to their site."

— *Terri Lenahan-Downs, Sponsorship Manager, The Louisville Zoo (Louisville, KY)*

| Article Designation Key: | Donors ▬▬▬ | Members ▬▬▬ | Volunteers ▬▬▬ |

26 Allow Donors to Check Their Gift History Online ▪ ▪ ▪

Many times, donors have a difficult time recalling the date of their last annual gift. To help donors do so, officials at Hamline University (Saint Paul, MN) came up with a website button that allows donors to easily e-mail a request for the date of their last gift.

"We had heard from alums that they didn't always remember their last giving date," says Karla Williams, director of annual giving programs. "We currently don't have self-service software for our alums to access their giving histories, so we came up with this idea as an interim step."

Although the button has only been on Hamline's website for a short period of time, Williams says it has brought in donor requests, particularly inquiries about company matching gift issues.

"While the response is just beginning to grow, its mere presence is a positive," Williams says. "It demonstrates we're available, we're interested in answering questions and we're responsive."

Content not available in this edition

Source: Karla B.A. Williams, Director, Annual Giving Programs, College of Liberal Arts, Hamline University, Saint Paul, MN. Phone (651) 523-2686. Email: kwilliams15@hamline.edu

27 Solicit Feedback Online ▪ ▪ ▪

The American Numismatic Association (Colorado Springs, CO) solicits feedback from its members on general and specific issues via an online form and posts a feedback summary on its website.

The association recently solicited feedback on proposed changes to its bylaws and convention exhibits. Because of the feedback they received on proposed changes to its draft bylaw proposals, the association made modifications to it.

Jay Beeton, deputy executive director for marketing and communication, says as a membership-based association, it's critical that they're in sync with what members want. "We need to not only take member feedback, but measure it and make it meaningful," he says. "We also need to ensure member feedback is considered when making policy decisions. Without that, you have failed your members."

While the online feedback form is the most convenient and least expensive way to solicit member feedback, Beeton doesn't like to limit it to that one method. The association also provides opportunities for members to share their feedback at coin shows, he says, where the executive director gives a "road show" laying out the association's future strategic initiatives and allows feedback opportunities, as well as at town hall meetings at its annual conventions.

"The town hall meetings give members a chance to express themselves and get the sense that the things they say matter," says Beeton.

They also offer members the opportunity to call or mail in their feedback, he says.

To view the association's member feedback form, visit www.money.org, click on "Communications" and then "Member Feedback."

Source: Jay Beeton, Deputy Executive Director for Marketing & Communication, American Numismatic Association, Colorado Springs, CO. Phone (800) 514-2646. E-mail: beeton@money.org

28 What Does Your Site Sound Like? ▪ ▪ ▪

Making your website sound like it comes from your organization will enable you to more effectively attract and inform members.

"By 'sound,' I'm referring to the way the content on your website reflects the way your organization wants to present itself," says Arthur Germain, principal and chief brandteller, Communication Strategy Group (East Northport, NY).

To assess how your website sounds, Germain says, ask:

❑ Does the content reflect our brand story today? Or is it just a rewritten version of content and photos from a former brochure?

❑ Do we greet site visitors with a tone that reflects our organization's personality?

❑ Do we use terms that are in-house or our organization's own lingo?

Based on your responses, you can take steps to create a website that tells a better sounding story:

1. **Tell it the way your members want to hear it.** Use terms members would expect when they visit your website. Ask a member what he/she thinks of your website content and design. Conduct a focus group of members or potential members.

2. **Skip the jargon.** "Nonprofits and other groups are notorious for using acronyms and industry terms," Germain says. If you need to use a term that may not be readily understood, explain it. Spell out acronyms the first time you use them.

3. **Use your voice to show you care.** Make a list of words that best reflect your organization. Then, use these words in ways that most effectively express the work of your organization through your website.

Source: Arthur Germain, Principal and Chief Brandteller, Communication Strategy Group, East Northport, NY. Phone (631) 239-6335. E-mail: info@gocsg.com

29 Create an Online Donor Spotlight Program ▬ ▬ ▬

A donor recognition technique that takes advantage of growing online usage and burgeoning technology is an online donor spotlight page.

Each month staff with the Domestic Violence Center (DVC) of Cleveland, OH, recognize donors on its website. It's a simple gesture with maximum results, says Linda Johanek, director of development.

"Donors really appreciate knowing that we value them, and that they are making a difference in domestic violence victims' lives," Johanek says "Everyone wants to know that their donation is being put to good use, it is much needed and appreciated."

Staff meet monthly to review gifts and events, and to suggest donors to recognize online based on:

- The uniqueness or creativity of the donation or event.

- The amount of time or energy involved.

- The number of people participating.

- The donor's history and his or her recognition history.

- The amount of the donation.

A staff member writes a brief article about the donor's fundraising activities or unique donation, and Johanek makes the final decision. Before publishing it online, DVC obtains the donor's permission.

Source: Linda Johanek, Director of Development, Domestic Violence Center, Cleveland, OH. Phone (216) 651-8484. E-mail: ljohanek@dvccleveland.org

31 Invite Bounce Backs on Your Site ▬ ▬ ▬

There are multiple reasons for inviting website visitors to provide you with input: It engages them in the work of your organization; it requires that they share their e-mail addresses; and their ideas and opinions may provide you with valuable insight.

Here are a few examples of statements and questions you may want to include or tailor to fit your organization's online presence:

- The first 50 people to send in correct answers to the following questions will receive a gift.

- Do you know the answers to these trivia questions about [name of organization]?

- We're looking for examples of.... If you can help, please reply.

- We're taking a vote on this important issue. Please share your response.

- Do you have news to share for the next issue of our newsletter? Click here to share it with us.

30 Encourage Your Volunteers To Form an Online Chat Group ▬ ▬

Looking to connect your volunteers and possibly attract younger persons to your volunteer ranks? Consider establishing an online chat group.

Online chat groups are free and easy to set up. Many of the main search engines, like Yahoo.com, offer this service.

Kathy Cahill, volunteer services coordinator, Lee County Parks and Recreation (Fort Myers, FL), says one of her groups of volunteers established and maintains an online chat group specifically for its location. The group is a great way for the volunteers to recruit within each other and stay connected, she says.

While the group is completely volunteer-run, Cahill did set some guidelines with the volunteers to make sure the content was appropriate. All content must be related to volunteers and/or wetland conservation.

Source: Kathy Cahill, Volunteer Services Coordinator, Lee County Parks and Recreation, Fort Myers, FL. Phone (239) 432-2159. E-mail: kcahill@leegov.com

32 Offer Endowment FAQs On Your Website ▬ ▬ ▬

Since many people are less familiar with endowments and how they work, it makes good sense to include frequently asked questions (FAQs) addressing endowment topics on your website.

Common endowment questions you might want to pose and answer include:

- ✓ What is an endowment?
- ✓ What's a named endowment?
- ✓ Why establish an endowment?
- ✓ What is the minimum amount necessary to establish a named endowment?
- ✓ What endowment funding opportunities are available?
- ✓ How is an endowed fund invested?
- ✓ Who oversees or manages the endowment?
- ✓ What is the current value of the endowment?
- ✓ What named funds currently exist and how are they being used?
- ✓ Can I establish a named endowment fund over time?
- ✓ Can I add to an endowed fund after my lifetime?
- ✓ How do I go about starting a named endowment fund?
- ✓ How does [name of your charity]'s endowment compare with the endowments of peers?

33   Put Your Volunteer Program Online ▬ ▬ ▬

What's required to get an online volunteer program off the ground?

In 2000, Pit Lucking, coordinator, Arizona State University Volunteer Services (Phoenix, AZ), learned firsthand what it takes to get an online program up and running.

"The online part of the program started because I wasn't successful in getting the agency information out to the university community," she says. After realizing the university website would be her best chance to reach their target audience, the online volunteer program was launched.

If your organization is considering an online volunteer program, Lucking offers this advice:

1. **Evaluate your program needs.** After the program's goals and strategy have been evaluated, see how the Internet can assist in accomplishing various needs. "This practice assures the online volunteer program is aligned with the program's goals," she says.

2. **Recruit those who need to establish and maintain the program.** 1) Decide what will go onto the site and design the structure (internal links) within it; 2) Write each page of the site (e.g., information, forms, links, etc.); 3) Decide if any pages should be secure and how visitors will have access; 4) Work with a Web designer to make the site attractive and easy to manage; 5) Put the site online and manage it; and 6) Evaluate visitor traffic — from where visitors are coming, how long they view various pages, how many return to the site, etc.

3. **Locate agencies that want to be part of the program.** Lucking says at the university she and another volunteer contacted community agencies about the online program. Agencies were offered free advertising space and participation in a free campus volunteer fair. Now the site covers the entire valley and is used by metropolitan Phoenix as a volunteer information source, says Lucking.

4. **Get the word out.** With a limited budget, Lucking says her program relies on passing out website business cards, community and agency word of mouth, and Internet search engines to increase awareness among potential volunteers.

Source: Pit Lucking, Coordinator, Arizona State University Volunteer Services, Academic Community Engagement Services, Phoenix, AZ. E-mail: pit.lucking@asu.edu

---

Online Volunteering
Opens Doors to Volunteers, Organizations

Is an online volunteer program right for your organization?

Lucking says their program has become a great volunteer resource for the Phoenix community with more than 350 agencies involved and more than 1,000 hits on the site weekly.

Lucking says many organizations and volunteers have turned to an online volunteer program for various reasons:

For the volunteer:

✔ If transportation is difficult.

✔ If they are limited physically.

✔ If people have commitments that require them to stay home yet they have the time and desire to volunteer.

✔ The freedom to schedule their time. Some individuals have schedules that allow them time to volunteer only when most agencies are closed.

For the organization:

✔ The online program reduces the cost of using paper and mail. A few clicks are more economical than spending resources for staff and supplies.

✔ It's easier to keep information updated.

✔ Online recruiting and volunteer registration provides accurate information about volunteers by storing it on electronic databases. This saves personnel time and improves program efficiency.

✔ The online program easily establishes electronic messaging as a powerful volunteer communications tool.

Content not available in this edition

34 Web Page Allows Donors to Compare Planned Gifts ▪▪ ▪▪ ▪▪

Help potential donors learn about planned gifts in the comfort of their own home or at their office with an interactive page on your website.

Alison Meyer, associate director of development, New Bedford Whaling Museum (New Bedford, MA), says her organization has used a "Compare Gifts" feature on its website to educate potential donors and encourage gifts.

"The Compare Gifts page informs donors of their options when considering a planned gift and which one might fit best for them," Meyer says.

The interactive Web page, hosted by The Stelter Company (Des Moines, IA), allows users to compare up to three planned gifts (e.g., a charitable gift annuity, a bequest in will or living trust, and an outright gift of cash).

The process is simple, Meyer says: Users select the gifts they would like to compare and are then directed to a page that illustrates the outcomes and assets for the chosen gifts. Additionally, users can read up-to-date articles about planned giving, learn the meaning of legal and fundraising jargon, as well as run gift calculations and request additional information.

The page "provides donors with a service, allowing

them to do their own research without an initial commitment, and then contact the organization only when they are comfortable in moving to the next step," she says. "It really helps our organization by bringing donors to the table who are educated and ready to have a serious conversation about planned giving."

Another benefit is the opportunity the service offers in terms of follow-up, Meyer says. "The Stelter Company lets us know when someone has been using the site extensively, so we can follow up with that individual. It is a great tool for learning who is interested in planned giving, without having to cold-call our donors on the subject."

The museum began offering the Compare Gifts site in 2006. At that time, Meyer says, "the museum was committed to having a planned giving program, but didn't have a staff person dedicated to it. The site's purpose was to bridge that gap."

In a recent five-month period, Meyer says, 20 visitors used the comparative gifts feature 44 times.

Source: Alison Meyer, Associate Director of Development, New Bedford Whaling Museum, New Bedford, MA.
Phone (508) 997-0046. E-mail: ameyer@whalingmuseum.org.
Website: www.whalingmuseum.org

35 Signing Up for Membership Online Has Its Advantages ▪▪ ▪▪ ▪▪

Enabling individuals to sign up for membership online will streamline the process for your members and your organization. It provides individuals with a convenient and efficient way to join your organization.

Alisha Smith, public relations and marketing specialist, American Paint Horse Association (Fort Worth, TX), shares her opinions on the value of online membership, saying:

1. **Enhanced customer service.** For members who require quick turnaround times, nothing will be faster or more accurate than joining online.

2. **Faster processing time.** Applicants know their information is received instantly.

3. **Error reduction.** Special features in the new system ensure data is entered completely and correctly. If data is missing or appears to be inaccurate, users will be prompted to re-enter the information. There will be no delay in processing time.

4. **Efficiency.** A properly completed application form ensures staff members can quickly complete the process of processing registrations. Applicants will know immediately if the information they are submitting needs to be updated or corrected.

5. **No postage costs.** Those who join online will normally complete the entire transaction online, eliminating the need for mailing.

6. **Safe and secure transactions.** The use of the latest encryption technology ensures all information submitted is safe and secure.

7. **Greater flexibility.** Joining online provides users with immediate access to the member-only portion of the online services, which includes access to pedigrees, performance records, foal registrations and so much more.

Source: Alisha Smith, Public Relations & Marketing Specialist, American Paint Horse Association, Fort Worth, TX.
Phone (817) 834-2742, ext. 220. E-mail: asmith@apha.com

36 Tout Chapter Activities Online ▪▪

What are you doing to promote chapters' activities on your website? Check out the alumni page of Marist College (Poughkeepsie, NY), www.marist.edu/alumni/, where you can find out what's happened or will be happening among its existing chapters.

37 Offer a Bequest Notification Form Online, by Other Means ▬

Persons bequeathing part of their estate do not usually notify the beneficiary of their plans.

A simple bequest notification form can help remind them to do so and could even move persons to add your cause to such plans.

A confidential bequest notification form posted online and mailed to alumni and parents of students at St. Charles Preparatory School (Columbus, OH) allows supporters to declare a financial provision in estate plans, says Douglas Stein, senior director of development and alumni affairs.

"This form allows our school to recognize now those individuals who declare their future intentions," Stein says. "It helps identify people (whose bequests) may not otherwise surface until after they have passed, and builds a meaningful relationship between the donor and school."

Stein says they have received nine completed forms in five years. When they do, they immediately follow up with a personal visit, phone call and letter.

For organizations considering such a form, he says to be prepared, as results may not be what you expect: "It's amazing to learn the people knocking around on your website."

Source: Doug Stein, Senior Director of Development and Alumni Affairs, St. Charles Preparatory School, Columbus, OH. Phone (614) 252-9288. E-mail: dstein@cdeducation.org

Content not available in this edition

38 Essential Elements of a Volunteer Web Page ▬ ▬ ▬

How does your volunteer Web page measure up? Four essential elements to include:

1. **A noticeable link from your agency's home page to your volunteer page(s)** — If website visitors land on your homepage, provide an obvious link to volunteer opportunities. Check out the index of links on the home page of Gulf Coast Jewish Family Services (Clearwater, FL) for an example (www.gcjfs.org).

2. **Easily accessible contact info** — For an example, see the Minnesota Historical Society's Web page (www.mnhs.org/about/volunteers).

3. **Location** — Offer a map or driving directions along with where to park and where to enter your offices once visitors arrive. Presbyterian Hospital of Plano (Plano, TX) offers location information and maps on its site (www.texashealth.org/hospitals). Click "Find Maps/Directions" and select "What Do You Want to Do?"

4. **Ways volunteers can help** — List types of volunteer opportunities. Enable website visitors to click on each item to receive more details about what's involved. Check out Harbor Medical Center's (Seattle, WA) Web page (www.uwmedicine.org/Facilities/Harborview/CommunityAndNews/Volunteer/Opportunities.htm).

39 Website Tip ▬ ▬ ▬

- Does your website include photos of volunteers in action? If not, find someone with a digital camera and take a few candid shots of your volunteers at work to post on your organization's website. With each photograph include a caption that highlights some of the perks — both tangible and personal — your volunteers receive from donating their time.

40 Engage Website Visitors ■ ■ ■

■ **Take periodic polls.** Asking visitors for their opinions on a specific topic is a great way to engage them. Plus, you may learn something from their collective responses. Polldaddy (www.polldaddy.com) is one free tool you can use to create surveys and polls for your website.

42 Showcase Opportunities For Involvement ■ ■ ■

How clearly does your website describe volunteer opportunities with which your members might want to become involved? Involving members as volunteers not only keeps them engaged and connected to other members, it helps you accomplish more than could otherwise be possible.

When describing volunteer opportunities on your website, remember to include the following information:

✓ Separate listing of volunteer opportunities available with brief summaries.

✓ Detailed position descriptions for each involvement opportunity.

✓ Calendar of scheduled meetings/events for each project.

✓ Particular qualifications for each involvement opportunity.

✓ Who to contact for more information regarding each volunteer opportunity (name, e-mail address and phone number).

Member Volunteer Opportunities

Below is a sampling of member organizations that offer volunteer opportunities on their websites:

Dayton (OH) Chamber of Commerce (www.daytonchamber.org) — Go to member connection and click on volunteering.

Minneapolis (MN) Institute of Arts (www.artsmia.org) — Click on get involved, then volunteer opportunities.

American Marketing Association (www.marketingpower.com) — Click on chapters, then volunteer opportunities.

---

41 List Endowment Options Online ■ ■ ■

Is the public aware of specific naming endowment opportunities that exist at your organization? Promote these naming opportunities by identifying them — and their costs — on your website.

Highland Park Independent School District (Dallas, TX) lists its named endowment opportunities online: visit, www.hpisd.org, select "Education Foundation," then "Endowment Campaign."

Another option is to list all existing named endowment funds. For an example, go to The Chesapeake Bay Maritime Museum's (St. Michaels, MD) website (http://cbmm.org) and click on "Giving to CBMM," then "Other Ways to Give." Showing named funds online serves to recognize existing endowment donors and encourage additions to those funds.

43 Include a Detailed Calendar Of Events Online ■ ■ ■

Officials with the Philadelphia Museum of Art (Philadelphia, PA) have found an inexpensive way to keep members up to date on the latest events and event details.

M.E. Bissert, communications coordinator, says the museum decided to add the user-friendly members' calendar in 2006 when they redesigned their website.

"Since many of our members utilize the Internet as an information resource, it was important for us to provide this service," says Bissert.

The calendar, which is updated as needed to provide members with up-to-the-minute information, is accessible to the museum's approximately 50,000 members. It features members-only events, programs, tours and public programs, including concerts, art history courses, lectures, family events and tours.

Bissert says the calendar also is a form of promotion. "Visitors are able to browse months in advance and view detailed program descriptions. They can search by event type. Having this information easily accessible creates interest and a buzz. We have included a 'forward to a friend' button, which sends the event information to a friend by the website visitor."

The institution also mails a monthly printed publication to their membership base to reach members who may not regularly use computers.

Source: M.E. Bissert, Communications Coordinator, Membership and Visitors Services Department, Philadelphia Museum of Art, Philadelphia, PA. Phone (215) 684-7853. E-mail: mbissert@philamuseum.org

44 Five Great Website Ideas ▪ ▪ ▪

Here are five great website ideas to help improve your volunteer program:

1. **Online volunteer training.** Deb Jones, extension specialist, 4-H Volunteer Development (Logan, UT), worked with a Web designer to create a fast, easy online program on volunteer training basics. Prospective volunteers input contact information at www.utah4-H.org and are immediately linked to training modules. Training is in steps to help them gauge their interest. It is also a marketing tool; contact information goes to appropriate 4-H contacts.

2. **Discussion forum.** Jones says 4-H volunteers across Utah wanted a way to bounce ideas off each other and ask questions. So she and Utah State University information technology staff developed a simple, interactive blog-like online discussion forum where volunteers can pose questions and get immediate responses.

3. **Resource library.** Jones assembled years worth of useful volunteer information into a searchable online database where visitors can look for and download 4-H-related documents, handouts, resources and materials.

4. **Volunteer opportunities guide** (www.bloomington.in.gov/volunteer), lists volunteer opportunities available through the City of Bloomington (IN) Network, says Bet Savich, director. The site is constantly updated and each listing provides a description of the organization, opportunity and contact information.

5. **Interest and skills index.** This works in conjunction with the guide, above, to help volunteers choose positions that best fit them. The index lists all areas of interest (e.g., environment, education, animals) and then links each area with the matching opportunities available.

Sources: Deb Jones, Extension Specialist, 4-H Volunteer Development, Logan, UT. Phone (435) 797-2202.
E-mail: deb.jones@usu.edu. Website: www.utah4-H.org
Elizabeth (Bet) Savich, Director, City of Bloomington Volunteer Network, Bloomington, IN. Phone (812) 349-3472.
E-mail: volunteer@bloomington.in.gov

46 Website Savvy ▪

The members-only section of your website should include compelling and continually changing information that attracts members to your site on a frequent basis.

45 Online Training Offers Member Benefits ▪

An online training program can provide a valuable benefit for your membership.

The National Glass Association (NGA) in McLean, VA, launched its online training program, MyGlassClass.com, in June 2006. It offers flat and auto glass companies a convenient, affordable and comprehensive resource for improving worker skills, enhancing workplace safety and achieving professional certification, says Deborah Schneider, senior manager of education and training. It also helps workers seeking to earn professional certification, improve technical skills and comply with training requirements.

What are the advantages of members taking online training? It's available 24 hours a day, seven days a week and students can work at their own pace. A computer and Internet access are the only tools needed to work on a course.

MyGlassClass.com is state-of-the-art because it's built on the GeoLearning Management System platform, a leader in the e-learning industry. "We also use Articulate software to present the courses, which provides a consistency in the look and feel of the courseware, but allows flexibility in graphics, audio, video, etc.," Schneider says.

The biggest challenge to hosting such a large online training program, Schneider says, is to handle the myriad duties involved in managing the system. To handle this challenge and others, Schneider suggests having support for the program from the top of the organization down. Also, put in place people and technical resources needed to manage the program before it begins.

Source: Deborah Schneider, Senior Manager, Education and Training, National Glass Association, McLean, VA.
Phone (703) 442-4890. E-mail: debis@glass.org

47 Convince Others To Create a Link to Your Site ▪ ▪

If you can't get everyone to learn about volunteer opportunities by visiting your website, maybe you can attract them by becoming visible on others' websites.

Make an all-out effort to convince businesses and other groups that have websites to include a link to your website. Whether you use direct mail, phone calls, face-to-face visits or a combination of those methods to get the job done, set a new links goal for yourself along with a deadline date. That way the project will become a priority that you can finish and put behind you. After all, once new links are in place, it's just a matter of responding to inquiries that reach your website.

48 Give Online Donors Choices ▨ ▨ ▨

A decision by university relations staff to create an online giving form resulted in a convenient giving tool for donors to Gonzaga University (Spokane, WA).

Dori Sonntag, director of annual giving, says her office, as well as fellow higher education institutions, have witnessed a trend away from other giving methods toward more online giving.

"We realized that we are an Internet society and in order to provide our donors with the best variety of options, we would have to get on board," and expand the online giving options available to donors, Sonntag says.

The form (www.applyweb.com/public/contribute?gonzagac) begins with the donor entering a donation amount (a $20 minimum; see graphic, below). Donors then select to apply the full amount to a single fund or multiple funds. Donors reenter the amount and choose a department/category from a drop-down menu.

Sonntag says these categories are updated annually according to the university's need. Some examples include: 2008 annual campaign, senior fund, performing arts, athletics, technology, residence hall renovations, mission-justice, etc.

Once a giving category is selected, another drop-down menu is available to select a specific fund applicable to that department/category (e.g., for the 2008 annual campaign donors can select from three choices: scholarships, College of Arts and Sciences; and Great Teachers Program).

Donors then choose a one-time contribution or a recurring donation (allowing the donor to select from monthly payments indefinitely, for 'x' amount of months or quarterly).

Through the online form, donors also can:

- designate if they would like to be recognized for their gift or remain anonymous;
- update their spouse and children information; and
- choose if their or their spouse's company will match their gift.

Online donors are asked to identify how they found the site (e.g., referred by a solicitation letter; student Telefund caller; university employee [with menu to select employee's name]; pledge reminder; e-mail communication; browsing the Web; or other).

Sonntag says during the 2006-2007 fiscal year (ending in May 2007), 355 donors contributed $105,000 through the online giving form. That was a 20 percent increase over the previous year. This year gifts through January 2008 have already surpassed last year's totals, with 243 donors giving $110,000.

Source: Dori Sonntag, Director of Annual Giving, Gonzaga University, Spokane, WA. Phone (509) 323-6149. E-mail: Sonntag@gonzaga.edu

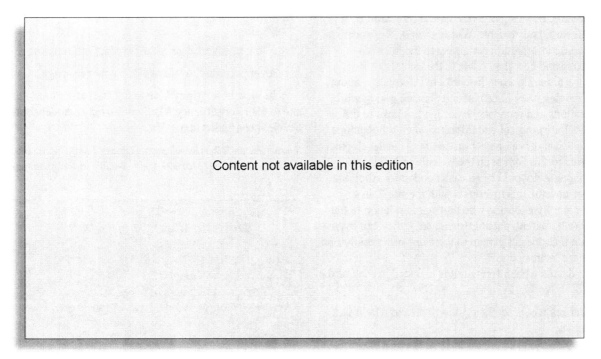

Content not available in this edition

Personalized Web Pages Draw in Prospects ▬ ▬ ▬

Personalized Web pages give prospective members a glimpse into your organization and just may inspire them to join.

At ASAE & The Center for Association Leadership (Washington, DC), "we implemented a PURL (Personalized URL) program and used a combination of direct mail and e-mail campaigns to encourage prospects to visit their own URL on the Web," says Melody Jordan-Carr, director, member relations. "We offered prospects the opportunity to join ASAE & The Center, to learn more about our organization and refer a colleague."

They scripted individual landing pages based on data prospects provided.

"The prospect was provided with a Web URL that incorporates their name into the address (e.g., http://join.asaecenter.org/Melody Jordan-Carr)," she says. "The program allowed us to integrate print and electronic products together," first sending prospects postcards, following up with letters and finally, e-mails including the personalized Web address.

The campaign, which targeted persons who had shown interest in the organization and former members who had not renewed memberships, brought in roughly 100 new members.

"Our meetings and expo team used the PURL idea to encourage registrations for the annual meeting. They advised us of the success of the program, so we pursued the project to acquire new members," says Jordan-Carr.

The PURLs, launched in September 2007, remained active through October, says Jordan-Carr. "After that point, we transitioned the program into what we call GURL (Generic URL), in which prospects are asked to go to www.join.asaecenter.org. Once there, the concept of the PURL is the same: Prospects are asked to identify themselves and learn more about our organization or they can opt to join immediately."

Source: Melody Jordan-Carr, Director, Member Relations, ASAE & The Center for Association Leadership, Washington, DC. Phone (202) 626-2853. E-mail: e.mcarr@asaecenter.org

 ## Online Giving: Reach Out to Varied Constituent Types ▬ ▬ ▬

Development officials at Trinity University (San Antonio, TX) target various types of donors through the "Supporting Trinity" portion of the university's website.

The website is segmented into six constituent groups: alumni, parents, friends, corporations and foundations, faculty and staff, and students. Within each of these mini-sites is specific information pertaining to the interests of each group and how they relate to the university. For example, the alumni portion has links to information about leadership giving, the phonathon and planned giving while the corporations and foundations portion has links to the business affiliate program and information on scholarships.

Jackie Sliker, development officer, says the development office moved to this format on the website in 2006.

"We thought it would be an easier and more efficient way for our constituents to interact with the site," says Sliker. "By simply choosing who they are in relation to the university (e.g., parent, alumni, friend, etc.), they can bypass information that doesn't pertain to them and more easily find what they are interested in."

Sliker details what information is included in each of the mini-sites:

- A description of what their gift will do and why it is important;
- Links to leadership giving information and giving programs specific to each group;

- A full explanation on the different ways to give to the university;
- Links to other parts of the Trinity website with information that might be of interest to that specific group;
- A link to advancement staff contact information;
- An opportunity to "Give Now" on every page.

To view how Trinity University staff tailor each mini-site to their constituency, visit www.trinity.edu/departments/development/index.htm.

Source: Jackie Sliker, Development Officer, Trinity University, San Antonio, TX. Phone (210) 999-8069. E-mail: jsliker@trinity.edu

 ### Website Idea ▬ ▬ ▬

Are you tailoring your website to the needs and interests of your volunteers?

Increasing numbers of nonprofit organizations — Wellesley College, Wellesley, MA (www.wellesley.edu/Resources/volunteer/index.html) — are including a volunteer tools page on their websites that volunteers can turn to for information and support.

52 Showcase Volunteer Opportunities With Online Slide Show ▪ ▪ ▪

Enticing potential volunteers with an online slide show of opportunities has helped St. Jude Children's Research Hospital (Memphis, TN) recruit volunteers for two years.

"It is a terrific, visual way for volunteers to learn more about our volunteer opportunities," says Kathryn Berry Carter, director of volunteer services. "Our slide show includes pictures of volunteers in action, a brief description of our available volunteer opportunities and requirements for each position."

She recommends the following tips for creating an online slide show:

- Take photos of volunteers in action as often as you can. Each of the 12 opportunities featured on the site rotate among multiple pictures. "The photos provide ... a mental picture of what the volunteer experience will be like," Berry Carter says. "They can visually see and imagine themselves participating as a volunteer."

- Think about your volunteer opportunities from the volunteers' perspective. What might interest them?

- Do not hesitate to include requirements. "Volunteers need to know what they are getting into and the expectations," Berry Carter explains.

- Keep the postings accurate and up to date.

St. Jude typically receives 30 volunteer applications each month. Although there is no way to determine a direct link between the slide show and the number of applications, Berry Carter says roughly half are online submissions, thereby indicating a likelihood of having viewed the slide show.

Source: Kathryn Berry Carter, Director of Volunteer Services, St. Jude Children's Research Hospital, Memphis, TN. Phone (901) 495-2277. E-mail: kathryn.berry-carter@stjude.org. Website: www.stjude.org

An online slide show for St. Jude Children's Research Hospital (Memphis, TN) features photos and descriptions of volunteering opportunities. (Screenshot photo by Laura Hajaar.)

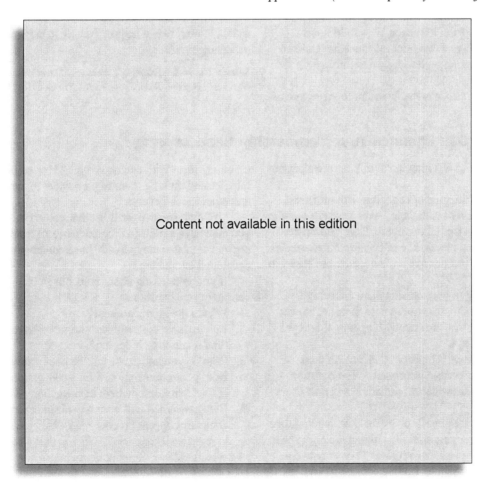

Content not available in this edition

53 Encourage Current, Potential Members With Online Video Tour ■ ■ ■

Go one step beyond the typical online tour of still photos and offer a video tour that grabs the attention of current and potential members alike.

The website for the Pony Express National Museum (St. Joseph, MO) has featured a two-minute video tour since the fall of 2007. Narrated by Cindy Sue Daffron, director of development, the video highlights different facets of the museum. A local television station that the museum regularly advertises with filmed and produced the video free and also aired it on local TV as part of its monthly spotlight segment.

"The video allows tour groups and members to see the progress in the museum and join in the progress of the museum going forward to 2010," when the museum will celebrate the 150th anniversary of the Pony Express, says Daffron.

She says there was no additional cost to have the video created beyond their normal monthly advertising fee for their television spots. The video is currently available via a link on the museum's homepage.

For the first-ever video tour for the museum, the TV crew spent several hours filming at the museum, including interviewing Daffron on camera, taking pictures of the museum displays and filming visitors in the gift shop. In addition, Daffron asked the television crew to film day-camp children and others throughout the museum. Daffron was given the opportunity to view the video throughout the production process.

The video tells the story of the museum, touching on his-torical information, points of interest and its most popular features, says Daffron, who adds: "I have met several people who visited the site and then decided to visit the museum after watching the video."

View the Pony Express National Museum's online tour at: www.ponyexpress.org

While the museum staff has not formally tracked how many persons were inspired to become members after view-ing the video tour, the director of development says she and her staff believe that the video has had an impact on motivat-ing people to join.

The video is also a beneficial tool for current members who are unable to visit as frequently as they would like, she adds, as it allows them to stay connected and reminds them how vital their support is to the museum's continued success.

Daffron says that while they currently do not track how many website visitors are viewing the online video tour, this would be a worthwhile feature to add.

She recommends that member organizations considering adding such an online feature reach out to local television stations to ask about policies and rates for nonprofits, as well as talk to members who may be able to assist in creating and producing a video.

Source: Cindy Sue Daffron, Director of Development, Pony Express National Museum, Saint Joseph MO. Phone (816) 279-5059.

54 Blogging Can Enhance Your Membership Base ■ ■ ■

Ever considered making blogging a part of your membership activity?

"The benefits of blogging or engaging with bloggers for any organization are considerable," says Terrance Heath, blogmaster, EchoDitto Inc. (Washington, DC). "Compared with other conventional media, like television or newspapers, blogging is relatively inexpensive and its effects are easier to measure."

To bring blogging to your organization, encourage members to blog about topics important to them. "Chances are some of your members are already blogging. Start by asking them," Heath says.

When gathering member information, collect their URLs along with their contact information. The question, "Do you have a website or blog?," should be a part of every membership form.

If your members are already blogging, start reading their blogs. "You may find opportunities to cultivate relationships with them and their readers," Heath says. "You may even start doing outreach to them by leaving comments on appropriate posts."

Other ways to reach your member bloggers include e-mailing them with exclusive updates or embargoed press releases and inviting them to participate in conference calls and other special events.

"If you have an e-mail list that you contact regularly, you may have a built-in blog audience," Heath says. "Your organization also may already have content that can be developed into a blog."

If you're thinking about launching a blog for members, consider these questions:

1. What's the blog's purpose?
2. Do you have the technical support who can dedicate the time required to blogging?
3. Who do you anticipate will be your primary bloggers?
4. Does your organization want a conventional blog or an online community where members have their own blogs?
5. How concerned will your organization be if negative comments appear on your blog? Will you require readers to register to comment? Will you post a comment policy?
6. What guidelines should be set?

Source: Terrance Heath, Blogmaster, EchoDitto Inc., Washington, DC. Phone (202) 449-5644. E-mail: terrance@echoditto.com

| Article Designation Key: | Donors ▨▨▨ | Members ▨▨▨ | Volunteers ▨▨▨ |

55 Include Board Bios on Your Website ▬ ▬ ▬

There are several reasons why you should publicly affiliate your board members with your organization: They add credibility to your cause; they take on greater ownership of your organization; and they deserve all of the accolades you can give them.

Showcase your board by including brief biographies and photos of each of them on your website. Make them interesting by sharing something of a more personal nature: what they enjoy doing in their spare time, what matters most to them or who's their most-admired hero and why.

Examples of Nonprofits Showcasing Their Board Members

KVMR, Nevada City, CA (www.kvmr.org/bod/index.html)

Cascade Land Conservancy, Seattle, WA (www.cascadeland.org/about-clc/board/board-bios)

Ballet Des Moines, Des Moines, IA (www.balletdesmoines.org/board-bios.html)

56 Online Calculator Simplifies Planned Giving ▬

Planned giving can be complicated and overwhelming. An online calculator is one way to take the confusion out of the process and better prepare donors for a conversation about planned giving.

"Calculators allow a potential donor to do some preliminary research prior to engaging a planned giving professional," says Jan Davis, director of planned giving, University of Central Arkansas (UCA) of Conway, AR, which offers an online calculator, shown at right. "In many cases, a donor is considering a planned gift as means for tax savings, and the calculator can give them a high-level idea of the charitable tax benefit they may receive."

To use the online calculator, created by Crescendo Interactive, Inc. (Camarillo, CA), potential donors simply go to www.ucagift.org, click "Gift Calculator" and:

- Select one of eight gift programs (Remainder Unitrust, Charitable Gift Annuity, etc.).

- Enter basic information (type of gift, gift date, age, amount, payout percentage, cost basis, payment frequency, etc.).

- View the results.

Website visitors can even create a personalized presentation that walks them through several gift programs, all of which help prepare them to meet with a planned giving advisor, says Davis.

"UCA wanted to provide the website as a tool for our alumni and friends to make them aware of the advantages of making a planned gift," Davis says. "In many instances, our current donors may be looking for some tax relief now and we want to ensure they know there are tools available to

them as they make their gifts to the institution. It's a win-win situation for the donor and the institution."

Source: Jan Davis, Director of Planned Giving, University of Central Arkansas, Conway, AR. Phone (501) 450-3470. E-mail: jdavis@uca.edu. Website: www.ucagift.org

Content not available in this edition

57 vMentors — A Program Making a Big Difference ▬ ▬ ▬

These days many nonprofit organizations use virtual volunteers — persons who work from a computer either on site or from home to fulfill a volunteer role.

One such nonprofit is the Orphan Foundation of America (OFA) of Sterling, VA.

OFA staffs 300 virtual volunteers to mentor teens with its vMentor program. This cognitive coaching matches teens in the OFA program with mentors who are interested in their success and guidance for their futures.

Founded in 1981, OFA serves thousands of foster teens across the United States. With the help of vMentors, 366 of those teens are given guidance by adult vMentor volunteers by way of e-mail dialogue, guiding the teens to make good decisions.

"We don't want the mentors to answer their questions, we want the mentors to guide the mentees to creating their own answers," says Lynn Davis, manager of partnership development.

How can your organization best utilize virtual volunteers?

- **Offer a structured training program** — Volunteers working within the vMentor program must complete an extensive virtual training program and participate in monthly trainings to volunteer as mentors to OFA teens. Mentors are trained to guide students to draw their own conclusions instead of offering them a direct answer to the problem.
- **Monitor all communications** — In OFA's case, all communications are done on secure portals and are monitored by staff to ensure the safety of the mentored teens.
- **Offer ongoing training and consistent contact with virtual volunteers** — vMentor volunteers participate in monthly trainings and support sessions headed by OFA staff to keep the program on track.

Participation in the vMentor program is a decision made by the teen. Teens mentored within the vMentor program are twice as likely to graduate than those who do not accept mentoring, says Davis, noting: "vMentors help our kids stay motivated to stay in college."

Lynn Davis, Manager of Partnership Development, Orphan Foundation of America, Sterling, VA. Phone (571) 203-0270. E-mail: ldavis@orphan.org. Website: www.orphan.org

58 Drive Members to Your Website With Branded Items ▬

Driving existing or potential members to your organization's website can be a challenge.

One way to get them there is to offer items branded with your organization's information, says Robb Hecht, media and marketing consultant, IMC Strategy Lab Consulting (New York, NY).

The most effective sales items for nonprofits and associations are branded t-shirts, caps, key chains and storage devices for documents like a CD ROM, Hecht says.

"Once you drive the potential member to your website, ask them to register with your site," Hecht says. The registration information is important to have so you can follow up with people. Send them your organization's regular e-mail newsletter, which is an effective way to attract members.

"From a marketing communications point, the key sales items are any of those which can drive the potential member to take action to get involved with the organization, even if it just means registering," Hecht says.

Successful sales items help to build relationships with members, donors and volunteers. These key items build a brand around the organization's cause and persuade people to join and participate.

Source: Robb Hecht, Media & Marketing Consultant, IMC Strategy Lab Consulting, New York, NY. Phone (800) 845-3779. E-mail: robb.hecht@imcstrategies.net

59 Online Certification Options Benefit Members ▬

Offering certification online provides many advantages for the organization and its members.

The National Association of Professional Pet Sitters (NAPPS) in Mount Laurel, NJ is beginning its online certification program early this year. One major benefit is that the online program is more affordable for members than the home-study course previously offered.

"Prior members who took the certification exam had to purchase the exam and reading materials," says Felicia Lembesis, executive director. "With the new certification test, members can access the reading materials in our virtual library." Members can complete one test area at a time and change any responses before their final submission.

"Beyond the cost benefit and ease of taking the test from home, less staff time is involved in fulfilling test orders, grading tests and providing results and certificates — this is handled online now," Lembesis says.

NAPPS creates awareness of the certification through the members-only section of its website, e-mail blasts and the quarterly member magazine. The organization set plans to unveil the new online program at its annual conference.

Source: Felicia Lembesis, Executive Director, National Association of Professional Pet Sitters, Mount Laurel, NJ. Phone (856) 642-4430. E-mail: flembesis@ahint.com

60 Medical Center Masters Online Volunteer Orientation ▬

To simplify the orientation process for you and your volunteers, offer it online.

Rather than requiring volunteers to sit through a face-to-face orientation session, an online orientation allows them to work at their own pace in a comfortable setting.

Plus, it makes tracking information much easier for your organization.

Volunteer coordinators at the University of Arkansas for Medical Sciences Medical Center (UAMS) of Little Rock, AR, began an online volunteer orientation a year ago.

Andrea Stokes, former volunteer coordinator and creator of its online orientation, says that when a volunteer's application is received electronically, he/she is asked to complete the online orientation. To do so, volunteers:

* Read through an online version of the volunteer manual. It covers topics ranging from safety codes to policies and procedures to the history of UAMS.

* Complete four tests and/or forms relating directly to material studied: HIPAA, confidentiality, safety and a volunteer contract.

* Receive an e-mail thanking them for completing the orientation and directing them to contact the volunteer department to schedule an interview.

"Essentially and ideally, all interested volunteers who have scheduled an interview have already completed their online orientation session and have an idea of the way UAMS operates, its history and its mission," Stokes explains.

To ensure a participant actually completes the orientation, she says:

* A database tracks each component of the orientation session.

* Applicants take tests to fully ensure they have read and understand the material.

* All volunteer applicants must interview with a staff member. During this time, the staff member evaluates the applicant's skill sets.

Source: Andrea Stokes, Clinical Research Promoter, Arkansas Children's Hospital, Little Rock, AR. Phone (501) 364-3309. E-mail: stokesandreac@uams.edu. Website: www.archildrens.org

---

Create a Successful Volunteer Orientation — Online

Andrea Stokes, former volunteer coordinator, University of Arkansas for Medical Sciences Medical Center (Little Rock, AR), offers the following advice for organizations interested in starting an online orientation process:

1. **Ignore the belief that online orientation only appeals to people in a specific age bracket.** "People from every generation are willing to try this out as long as you are patient with your instructions and make your module easy to find and easy to understand," she explains.

2. **Be meticulous when editing your website and orientation module.** Stokes says it is important to create a friendly and welcoming look. Additionally, avoid spelling and grammatical errors.

3. **Be prepared to edit and update.** "There is nothing worse than a website that hasn't been edited in more than a year," Stokes says. "If your uniforms have changed, change your pictures. If your confidentiality statement has been revised, don't forget to revise it in your orientation materials. You don't want to mislead volunteers."

4. **Use lots of guinea pigs.** Stokes recommends going through the materials monthly to make sure everything is working properly and is user-friendly.

5. **Invest in a good database.** "Volunteer tracking is essential to maintaining any volunteer program, especially when you are using an online system that may attract individuals who never become volunteers," Stokes says. "Keep all records and, if you can, track all correspondence you make with potential applicants via e-mail, your website, telephone, etc. It's helpful to have those records when you hear from them again."

61 Pressrooms Have Multiple Benefits ■ ■ ■

Could your organization and its members benefit from an online pressroom? More member organizations are putting pressrooms on their websites. Meagan Stangle, communications specialist, Kellen Communications (Atlanta, GA), answers questions about online pressrooms:

What's the purpose?

"The pressroom provides the media and consumers up-to-date news and information about an organization," says Stangle. "The media can access the pressroom at any time, providing them with relevant information without having to spend a lot of time searching the Web or trying to find the appropriate contact person."

Media rooms become especially beneficial during a crisis. An organization can channel reporters to the individuals most prepared to answer questions about a specific topic.

How do members benefit?

"A pressroom allows members to see the proactive efforts an agency is undertaking on the organization's behalf," Stangle says.

Media rooms can serve as a "brag board" for the organization's achievements. In addition, post photos of members in the association's leadership, along with their biographies.

"Some members may not fully grasp the purpose of public relations and the pressroom may help members recognize the benefits of a public relations program," Stangle says.

What's involved in set up?

The first step is to decide which materials should be included in the pressroom for your organization. "Some pressrooms contain the basic information about an organization such as fact sheets and brochures," Stangle says. "Others are updated frequently with the latest press releases and media pick up."

After deciding on materials for the website, the organization can have its webmaster post the materials on the designated area of the website.

What can you include?

A pressroom can include various items such as background information, fact sheets, white papers, e-newsletters, articles, brochures, frequently asked questions (FAQs), media contacts and press releases. Include a sign-up link so reporters can opt in to get on your organization's distribution list.

Is this time consuming to maintain?

A pressroom doesn't have to be time consuming, but do remove documents once they're no longer relevant. Add those current documents as they become available. "It's a good rule of thumb to ensure each document posted has a relevant title and keywords in the source code," Stangle says.

What are other good tips and advice?

"It's important that a pressroom is kept up to date," Stangle says. "If the media discovers you as a reliable information source on a specific topic, they may frequent your website's pressroom for ideas and additional information.

"An out-of-date pressroom will not only dissuade the media from visiting your website, but may result in the printing of incorrect information about your organization's topic."

When posting articles, keep in mind copyright restrictions and only post a link to the article publisher's website. Don't republish article content from other media on your Web page.

The pressroom should be displayed prominently on your organization's website so the media doesn't need to search your site to find the information they're seeking.

Source: Meagan Stangle, Communications Specialist, Kellen Company, Atlanta, GA. Phone (678) 303-3061. E-mail: mstangle@kellencompany.com

62 Strategies for Increasing Your Donor Participation Rate ▬ ▬ ▬

What strategies do you have in place to increase your donor participation rate?

One tool used by Pomona College's Annual Giving office (Claremont, CA) is a thermometer on its website (www.pomona.edu/annualfund/) to point out the college's alumni participation rate goal and where it is to date.

"Since we are deadline-focused, having a thermometer on our website is a good way to publicize these two goals and show our donors how their gifts help us reach our goals by our annual deadline," says Craig Arteaga-Johnson, director of annual giving. "The transparent thermometer provides donors with a basic context for their giving (e.g., How much is being raised? Is there a deadline for giving?)"

The thermometer shows the college's fiscal year annual fund goals ($4.5 million for 2007-2008) along with participation rate. A small section below the columns states the annual fund goal specifics (e.g., participation goal, participation rate, dollar goal and dollars raised) as well as the date the information was last updated. An option to make a gift online is also available directing visitors to an online giving form.

In addition to the thermometer, Arteaga-Johnson identifies three other strategies used to meet their participation rate goal:

1. **Compelling messaging.** Communications are focused on the messages that are most compelling to their audiences and describe how their gifts make a difference.

2. **Multiple types of communication.** Audiences are reached with multiple types of communication (e.g., phone calls, letters, e-mails, postcards and the website).

3. **Repeated requests.** Constituents are contacted multiple times throughout the fiscal year to make a gift. They receive a letter every few months, as well as phone and e-mail communications.

In 2007, Pomona College received some 1,200 gifts online, totaling more than $300,000.

Source: Craig Arteaga-Johnson, Director of Annual Giving, Pomona College, Claremont, CA. Phone (909) 621-8142. E-mail: craig.arteagajohnson@pomona.edu

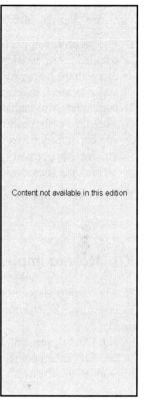

Content not available in this edition

63 Create an Online Advertising Service ▬ ▬ ▬

Offer members a high-tech perk: advertising space on your website.

In September 2008, staff with the Monroeville/Monroe County Chamber (Monroeville, AL) began offering members the option of purchasing advertising space through the chamber's website. Members can choose from seven advertising options, from a homepage banner ad ($500 annually) to a relocation page ad ($420 annually).

ECTown USA (Quincy, CA) designed the page on the chamber's website that showcases online advertising options, says Sandy Smith, executive director. The website design company, Appleby Arts (Boulder City, NV) creates the member ads. Cost to create each ad is $30 without flash and $60 with flash.

The chamber's goal is to sell $3,000 in banner ads within the next year.

"The online advertising is a great opportunity for us to promote our local businesses, events and organizations, and everything is just a click away," says Smith.

Plans are to create a promotional campaign using radio, newspaper and online mediums to make all members aware of the new online advertising system, she says.

Smith emphasizes finding the right company to work with when designing an online advertising system for your members: "Find a company that is customer responsive and that specializes in your type of business. One reason we chose ECTown is that they do a lot of work with chambers. They wake up every day thinking of ways that chambers can assist their members and be a better front door to their communities."

Source: Sandy Smith, Executive Director, Monroeville/Monroe County Chamber, Monroeville, AL. Phone (251) 743-2879.

| Article Designation Key: | Donors ▬▬ | Members ▬▬ | Volunteers ▬▬ |

64 Three Ways to Recruit Volunteers Online ■ ■ ■

Have you ever considered using the Web to recruit volunteers? Following is a list of ways to utilize the Internet to increase your volunteer numbers.

1. **Use an online opportunities list.** Do you include a detailed position description? The more information you can give the better. Attention spans are short; give the surfer as much information as possible, right from the beginning. Also include your e-mail address or create a separate e-mail address just for online recruitment so your current inbox doesn't get overloaded. Most volunteer opportunity lists are free, so put opportunities on multiple sites.

2. **Make sure your website is recruitment friendly.**

Put a visible link, like a highlighted box, to your volunteer page on every page of your website, home, other departments, etc. Beyond that have the link list available, volunteer opportunities and an online application. Make signing up to volunteer online as easy as possible.

3. **Create a newsgroup.** A newsgroup is like an online community where its members can chat, receive notices, etc. You can create your own site for your volunteers and direct prospective volunteers to it. Newsgroups can also be searched based on topic. Check out http:// groups.google.com for an online tour and instructions to set up your own group.

65 How to Implement a Successful Virtual Meeting ■ ■ ■

Virtual meetings electronically connect partners, clients and associates from any location while saving on gas and travel costs.

Jim Bandy, president, Brainband Technology Services (Dallas, TX), offers points to keep in mind to make your online meeting effective:

1. **Choose a program that fits your needs.** Popular virtual meeting platforms available for purchase include Microsoft Office Live Meeting, Adobe ConnectNow and Cisco WebEx. Free software such as Mikogo and FreeConferenceCalls incorporates webinar capabilities. Bandy says the program you choose should have a few key features:

   ✓ **Whiteboard** — This feature allows the presenter to edit documents and other materials as in a traditional meeting, letting attendees see markups in real time.

   ✓ **Chat** — This tool could display messages for everyone to see or show private instant messages between two people, allowing attendees to communicate with the presenter and other participants without interrupting the meeting's flow.

   ✓ **Control transfer** — In online meetings, it will be useful for the presenter to be able to transfer mouse and keyboard control to another team member in case further explanation is needed.

2. **Do a run-through.** "People respect a well-run meeting, so become familiar with the tools and applications in your online conference software beforehand in order to avoid embarrassing moments," says Bandy. Plan details, including scheduling the meeting at a convenient time

for everyone (keep time zones in mind) and planning a brief time for questions and answers.

3. **Don't over-invite.** Keep the invitation list short and only notify those whose attendance is mandatory. Send invitations well enough in advance and send a reminder the day before to ensure a prompt start. "Gathering the right people as opposed to the largest crowd will make your meeting more effective and increase the attentiveness and interaction in the meeting," says Bandy.

4. **Send an e-mail.** Sending a well-written e-mail will remind participants of the upcoming meeting and give them an idea about topics to be covered. When forming your e-mail, keep these things in mind: Make the subject line attention grabbing; keep the copy conversational; and call out the benefits of the meeting and how it will serve the attendees. Also, be sure the time zone associated with the scheduled online meeting time is made clear in the e-mail. The end of the e-mail should include a call to action, motivating recipients to RSVP.

5. **Keep it interesting.** Spend the majority of the meeting interacting with attendees and sharing information of interest and benefit to all participants. Don't waste time on objectives that can be accomplished via e-mail or a phone call. Collaborate as a group on brainstorming, decision-making, team building, etc. Incorporating slides from Microsoft PowerPoint and documents from Microsoft Word or Excel helps break up the routine of a lecture and keep people visually focused.

Source: Jim Bandy, President, Brainband Technology Services, Dallas, TX. Phone (972) 231-7128. E-mail: jbandy@brainband.com

66 Increase Online Giving ■ ■ ■

To increase online giving, develop ways to involve visitors with your website. Make your website involvement rich by adding features such as:

- Members-only interactive groups
- Online surveys
- Online threaded discussion groups
- Online chat groups or bulletin boards
- Chat sessions with experts
- Online book clubs
- Other affinity groups

68 Get Rid of Paperwork And Streamline Recruitment ■ ■ ■

Have you embraced online recruitment yet? No paper work, no hard files and no formal interviews, just putting an interested volunteer to work in a couple of days.

That's how it works for Kris Cord, partnership and volunteer center coordinator, Poudre School District (Fort Collins, CO), and staff. It has to because more than 8,000 people volunteer for the school district. With numbers like that, Cord says it was impossible to keep the hard files consistent.

Which is why she spent months researching software and decided to go with Samaritan's E-Recruiter software. The entire recruitment process is done online, from any computer.

When a potential volunteer navigates to Poudre School's volunteer page, they click a button to sign up. Screens come up asking the volunteer about contact information, interests, skills and availability. As soon as the volunteer clicks send they receive an e-mail letting them know someone will get in touch with them soon.

The volunteer's information goes right to a linked organization that performs the background check. Unless it is during the busy recruitment time, the checks are back in 24 hours. Otherwise, it is two to three days. The volunteer's electronic information goes into the requested school's file and the school's building volunteer coordinator takes it from there, either with an e-mail or a phone call to the volunteer.

No paperwork, the right questions, a speedy return and the right software have made online recruiting a breeze for Cord. Every year volunteers are asked to edit and update their online information to make sure the system stays accurate.

Source: Kris Cord, Partnership and Volunteer Center Coordinator, Poudre School District, Fort Collins, CO. Phone (970) 490-3207. E-mail: kcord@psdschools.org

67 Get More Milage From Your Website ■ ■ ■

Logging the hours of off-site volunteers usually requires a lot of paperwork, including the signature of the volunteer's immediate supervisor. Elaine Hanson, director, RSVP, Waldorf College (Forest City, IA), felt the process was condescending for adult volunteers.

The college's webmaster and IT department explained she could integrate an online posting system to her existing website. Now, each volunteer supervisor receives a pin number and can log their volunteer's hours in from any location.

Hanson says the information is kept in an account that is saved on the server. A volunteer or student helps download and record the hours. An update is done every fall to add or change pin numbers. The online tracking also meets all of her federal guidelines.

If your organization does not have a webmaster or IT department, ask your local college or university if students are available for a Web internship or ask a local computer business to assist.

Source: Elaine Hanson, Director, RSVP, Waldorf College, Forest City, IA. Phone (641) 585-8294. E-mail: hansone@waldorf.edu

69 Website Assessment Survey Gets Member Feedback ■ ■ ■

What do members think of your website? What might be missing, in their opinion? How do they think your website might be improved?

Include an assessment survey on your website to encourage feedback. Although the majority of visitors won't respond to the survey, others will provide useful insights. They may offer overlooked suggestions — making your address and phone number more easily accessible — or advice on catering to member interests. Have a procedure in place for providing immediate and meaningful feedback to those who participate.

Website Assessment Examples

Here are a few examples of website assessment surveys:

- **Washington Trails Association (Seattle, WA)** — www.wta.org
- **Cleveland Clinic (Cleveland, OH)** — http://cms.clevelandclinic.org/sarcoidosiscenter/body.cfm?id=44
- **St. Paul Schools (St. Paul, MN)** — http://rea.spps.org/SPPS_REA_Website_Survey.html
- **Kansas City Public Library (Kansas City, MO)** — www.kclibrary.org/promos/websurvey/questions.cfm

70 **Ways to Protect Member Privacy** ▬

Whether you represent an alumni association, chamber of commerce or art museum, it is important to take appropriate steps to protect your members' privacy.

Diane Bruhl, director, membership and marketing division, American Bar Association (ABA) in Chicago, IL, says with the new millenium technological changes (e.g., e-mail communications and updating member information online), they decided to radically modify the original 1978 privacy policy.

To make the privacy policy more accessible and transparent to its 413,108 members, the ABA placed the statement online in 2000. The statement addresses e-mail privacy, e-mail information gathered by the ABA and disclosure information.

Bruhl says the ABA takes additional steps to ensure member privacy:

1. **Database/membership system security.** To reduce the threat of information theft, only certain staff members have authorization to access the membership database.

2. **Website security.** The security system prevents unauthorized access and changes to member information. Members with authorized passwords are able to log in for address updates, transactions, member directories, etc.

3. **Seed name and decoy monitoring are put on internal and third-party mailings.** Members are given predetermined decoy names that are attached to all lists so the member receiving mailings can determine who sent them. This monitoring allows ABA to track its lists sold to third parties to make sure information is not used without proper authorization.

4. **Credit card information disappears from the system once a transaction clears.** Members' credit card information is not stored by the ABA. Instead, when a member uses their credit card information, a program encrypts the information and removes it upon approval.

Source: Diane Bruhl, Director, Membership and Marketing Division, American Bar Association, Chicago, IL. Phone (312) 988-5519. E-mail: BruhlD@staff.abanet.org

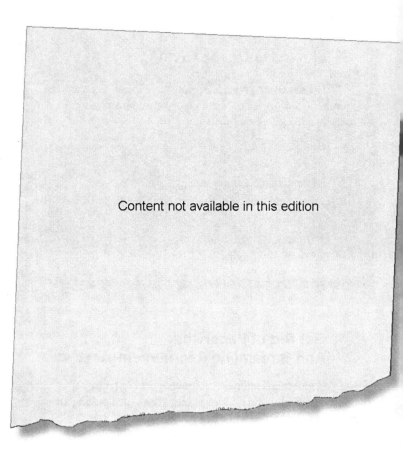

Content not available in this edition

Members Refer to Online Privacy Policies

According to a recent member survey conducted by The Nature Conservancy (Arlington, VA), members use the Web, specifically the online privacy policy, to learn more about the organization, what it does and how it functions.

Begoña Vázquez-Santos, director, membership fundraising, says the survey showed 42 percent of members researched the agency online before making a donation and 21 percent consulted a charity watchdog before supporting The Nature Conservancy. The members identified the privacy policy as one of the areas they researched.

"The privacy policy and certifications such as Verisign Secured Sign are tools we use to explain the steps we take to ensure the member's personal and donation-related information is secure with us," says Vázquez-Santos.

Other nonprofits that have online privacy statements include:

*   **The American Mathematical Society** — www.ams.org/ams/privacy.html
*   **Bedford Area Chamber of Commerce** — www.bedfordareachamber.com/privacy.htm
*   **Wisconsin Alumni Association** — www.uwalumni.com/privacypolicy.aspx

Source: Begoña Vázquez-Santos, Director, Membership Fundraising, The Nature Conservancy, Arlington, VA. Phone (703) 841-8779. E-mail: bvazquez@tnc.org

Article Designation Key: Donors ▬▬▬ Members ▬▬▬ Volunteers ▬▬▬

71 Use Your Website to Promote Endowment ▣

Have you considered designating a page on your website to educate and encourage your constituents to consider certain giving options? That's what officials with The Kansas City Public Library (Kansas City, MO) elected to do after receiving an unexpected endowment gift from a donor.

In 1985, David Taggart named the library as beneficiary of a $40,000 bequest. This planned gift allowed the library to start an endowment fund which has grown into several funds and today totals more than $5 million.

"Mr. Taggart is an unknown hero of the library and his story is a testament of quiet appreciation for an institution such as a library that can be of benefit throughout a person's life," says Claudia Baker, director of development.

The inspiration of Taggart's gift encouraged the library to create a library page on its website in 2002 that highlights and answers common questions about endowment gifts, says Baker: "For us, endowment is a part of the whole development/fundraising approach. We want to make sure our patrons and friends are aware of the full range of giving opportunities."

The website (www.kclibrary.org/support/endowment/cfm) addresses:

- What an endowment is.
- Why the library's endowment funds are so important.
- If it's possible to designate a gift to a specific endowment.
- How one can help the endowment grow.

In 2007 the endowment page received 1,176 hits. Since launching the page the library has received four bequests totaling $108,000. Baker says while these gifts cannot solely be attributed to the website page, they are a result of a collaboration of website visits, library patronage, event participation and other communications.

Source: Claudia Baker, Director of Development, Kansas City Public Library, Kansas City, MO. Phone (816) 701-3518. E-mail: claudiabaker@kclibrary.org

Content not available in this edition

72 Virtual Volunteers, a Practical Option for Many ■ ■ ■

Scheduling time to volunteer can be difficult. If only opportunities were available after work or after the kids went to bed. Now they are, thanks to virtual volunteering.

Rachel Thuermer, program director, Dare to Dream Theatre, Inc. (Manitowoc, WI), says her organization has turned to virtual experiences to make volunteering easier and more accessible. Additionally, she says, virtual volunteering has opened the door to a much larger pool of volunteers with specific interests and skills.

"Through virtual volunteering we can not only spread the mission of our organizations outside our communities, but also find amazing volunteers who we would otherwise never had the opportunity to work with," Thuermer says.

Although the advantages are many, Thuermer says virtual volunteering is not without its challenges. For instance, it requires an extra time commitment for volunteer managers as timeliness and motivation can be difficult for volunteers at a distance.

"The volunteer manager should keep in constant communication with the virtual volunteer to ensure projects are getting completed and done well in a timely manner," she says.

Additionally, Thuermer cautions, "Not all people can be effective virtual volunteers. You need a skilled, really motivated, self-disciplined person who is good at time management and has a passion for the organization's mission."

Source: Rachel Thuermer, Program Director, Dare to Dream Theatre, Inc., Manitowoc, WI. Phone (920) 682-2104. E-mail: daretodreamtheatre@msn.com

73 Offer Members E-cards as Part of Online Services ■ ■ ■

Looking for new online services to offer members? Consider free e-cards, a member benefit that also helps you share your organization's name with a wider audience.

Members of the Mizzou Alumni Association of the University of Missouri (Columbia, MO) have been sending e-cards from the association's website for nine years.

"Offering e-cards is an easy and fun way to engage alumni and assist them in connecting or reconnecting with friends and classmates," says David Roloff, director, membership and marketing.

Alumni choose from nine e-cards, including happy birthday messages, anniversary congratulations and other sentiments. Members can send an unlimited amount of cards at no charge once they log in on the association's website.

An online services vendor, iModules, helped develop and manage the feature.

"We design the card graphics and decide what cards to post," Roloff says, noting: "Since there are so many e-cards out there, we decided just to go with what we felt was best and fit into the module's specs."

He says that while the association does not regularly track numbers of e-cards sent, 2007 statistics show that on average, members send roughly 600 cards a month.

"We occasionally promote the use of the e-cards on our homepage and in our alumni e-newsletter," says Roloff. "When we do that, it drives traffic way up."

By branding the e-cards with your organization's name and logo, you are allowing your members to stay in touch with valued friends while also supporting your organization, Roloff says. "Development of any e-card should include a way for the recipient to return to the association's website to learn more about the organization and/or to send their own e-card."

Source: David Roloff, Director, Membership & Marketing, Mizzou Alumni Association, University of Missouri, Columbia, MO. Phone (800) 372-6822. Website: www.mizzou.com

The Mizzou Alumni Association (Columbia, MO) features free e-cards alumni can send once logging on to the alumni website.

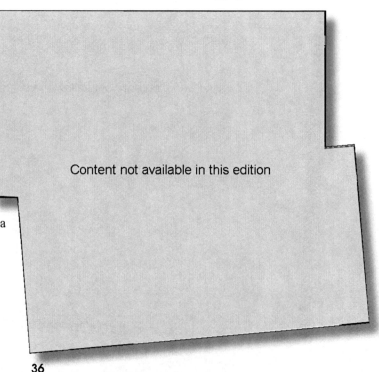

Content not available in this edition

Article Designation Key: Donors ▬ Members ▬ Volunteers ▬

74 The Ins and Outs of an Online Gift Planner ▪

The San Antonio Area Foundation (San Antonio, TX) offers an online resource for potential donors, as well as for financial advisors and other charitable organizations. The Build Your Gift planner, a service offered by the Stelter Company (Des Moines, IA), allows users to take a brief quiz to determine what type of gift best suits them.

"There are many charitable gift vehicles and the Build Your Gift planner helps donors decide which vehicle might be right for them," says Kathleen Finck Smudy, the foundation's director of planned giving. "Armed with this information, they can then intelligently discuss their options with their financial advisor and with our staff.

"Financial advisors also take advantage of this tool to gather information about charitable giving options and to narrow the choices they will discuss with their clients," Smudy says. "Other charitable organizations can also utilize the Build Your Gift planner with their donors. It is great to be able to support the charities and financial professionals in the San Antonio area in this way."

The planner takes participants through a series of questions and, based on their answers, suggests charitable gift vehicles that fit the donor's situation.

The online tool highlights lifetime gifts such as charitable remainder unitrusts, charitable annuity trusts, charitable gift annuities and deferred charitable gift annuities; gifts of different types of property such as real estate, tangible personal property, securities, cash and business interests; and estate gifts such as bequests and gifts of retirement plan assets and life insurance made by naming the charity as beneficiary.

When the online tool suggests a gift vehicle, she says, the donor is provided information about that particular vehicle, such as how it operates, what variables to consider, what kind of tax benefits it can provide and how it benefits the area foundation.

"With more people having access to the Internet and becoming self-directed, a gift planner is a great tool to connect your organization with a wider donor base," Smudy says. "These days, consumers want to inform themselves before making decisions or even consulting with experts. We provide objective information for our donors and financial planners, enabling them to intelligently discuss charitable giving. The planner is also very quick and can provide suggestions and information much faster than a human being."

Source: Kathleen Finck Smudy, Director of Planned Giving, San Antonio Area Foundation, San Antonio, TX. Phone (210) 242-4744. E-mail: ksmudy@saafdn.org. Website: www.saafdn.org

75 Promote Member Businesses With Website of the Month Feature ▪ ▪ ▪

Visit the website for the South Wayne County Regional Chamber (Taylor, MI) and you'll notice a feature that highlights an individual member's website.

Chamber staff select one member's website to feature on the chamber homepage each month, says Sandy Mull, vice president. Doing so, she says, both encourages members to create a website that promotes their business and brings them more attention.

Chamber staffers rate member sites on appearance, user-friendliness and if a site entices a visitor to want to go beyond the homepage. Mull recommends having clear rules for the selection process so that members who are not selected do not feel slighted.

The chamber also allows members to nominate sites they feel are worthy of attention. Members can even nominate their own sites, but a member website can only be featured once every 12 months.

"We're always looking for services we can provide for our members," says Mull. "'Website of the Month' is just one more way to promote our member's businesses."

Source: Sandy Mull, Vice President, South Wayne County Regional Chamber, Taylor, MI. Phone (734) 284-6000. E-mail: Sandy@swcrc.com. Website: www.swcrc.com

76 Include Volunteer Descriptions On Your Website ▪ ▪ ▪

You already know it's wise to develop job descriptions for volunteer positions. They help would-be volunteers know exactly what's expected of them.

Why not post descriptions on the volunteer segment of your website?

Officials with the Nashville Ronald McDonald House (Nashville, TN) offer descriptions for both family and group volunteers at www.rmhnashville.com/volunteer/index.html. The PDF format descriptions spell out scheduling shifts, age requirement, term commitment, training expectations, medical requirements, background check requirements and more.

For more info: Nashville Ronald McDonald House Charities of Nashville, Nashville, TN. Phone (615) 343-4000. E-mail: volunteer@rmhnashville.com

77 Drive Potential Donors to Your Website ▰ ▰ ▰

Your organization's website features valuable information, as well as an easy and secure online donation process. But what good is the site without traffic?

Here are six ways to drive potential donors to your organization's website:

1. **Encourage referrals.** Include a Refer-a-Friend option on your website that lets visitors send an e-mail to friends suggesting they check out your website (we all know a friend's suggestion truly means something!). Consider the same option for your e-newsletter.

2. **Be a tease.** If your organization does not have a blog, start one. Blogs are a great way to share your message. To get people to visit your site, entice them with a teaser. For instance, if your website features informational articles, post the first few lines on your blog, along with a link to your website to read the rest of the story.

3. **YouTube.** Ask a local college to help make a short video or develop a video campaign to post on YouTube. Be sure to check out YouTube's nonprofit program (www. youtube.com/nonprofits) and create your own channel.

When making the video mention or show your organization's web address several times.

4. **Offer incentives.** Give people a reason to visit your site. For instance, encourage persons to register for a drawing. Or, pose a question or quiz in your newsletter with directions to visit your website for the answer.

5. **Trade links.** Ask other nonprofit organizations or event sponsors to include a link to your website from theirs. Don't forget to ask that CEO on your board of directors to post a link on his/her company site.

6. **Apply for a Google Grant** (www.google.com/grants). Recipients receive at least three months of free advertising up to $10,000 per month. As a recipient, you'll choose keywords relevant to your organization. When Google users search for those keywords, your AdWords ad will appear. Users can click on the ad and go directly to your website.

78 Highlight New Members On Your Website ▰ ▰ ▰

Showcasing new members online is a great way to introduce and welcome them to your organization.

Members new to the Cleburne Chamber of Commerce (Cleburne, TX) have taken center stage on its website for seven years. When staff enter a new member's information into the database, the software program immediately updates the website's new member section. Information remains on the page for 30 days.

Chamber officials use software created by the chamber-driven software company, Steve Boyles & Associates, Inc. (www.sbainc.net). A staff member is designated to update the database with new member information immediately after the member joins. Once in the system, new members' business names and contact information are listed in an online new member section, flagged with "new" and appear as a scrolling list on one side of the page.

Cathy Marchel, chamber president, says the website gets up to 90,000 hits a month.

"Our job is to promote and refer our members," she says. The online member spotlight "is something special for a new member. In most cases they are a new business. This gives them the extra exposure they need when joining the chamber."

Source: Cathy Marchel, President, Cleburne Chamber of Commerce, Cleburne, TX. Phone (817) 645-2455.
E-mail: cmarchel@cleburnechamber.com.
Website: http://members.cleburnechamber.com

79 Offer Links to Members' Websites ▰ ▰ ▰

Although it doesn't make sense for every type of member organization, consider the possibility of including links to your members' personal or business websites on your own website. Doing so may be considered a significant benefit to some of your members.

Organizations Offering Links to Members' Sites

Kansas Auctioneers Association —
www.kansasauctioneers.com/members/sites.php

Citizens for the Arts in Pennsylvania —
www.paarts.org

The Galpin Society — www.galpinsociety.org

---

80 Simple Show-and-tell Can Add to Web Traffic ▰ ▰ ▰

Everyone knows what donors want, especially in today's economy — results.

Spotlight those results by adding one simple line to thank-you letters, pledge forms, pre-printed receipts and other donor correspondence. For example, staff with the United Way of Snohomish County (Everett, WA) includes this line on pledge forms and other publications: "See how your donation is making an impact at www.uwsc.org."

Regardless of the wording you use, this simple way of connecting your donors to your cause can boost website traffic while feeding your donors what they crave: results.

81 Feature Friends Groups on Website to Gain Volunteer Attention ▬ ▬ ▬

UC Santa Cruz (UCSC) of Santa Cruz, CA, has devoted a page of its website highlighting opportunities for students, staff, faculty and community members to get involved through service — both on and off campus. Listed on the Volunteer Opportunities page of the site are 14 groups offering volunteer activities called Friends Groups and five other programs such as the alumni association.

Friends Groups are officially recognized campus support groups and are generally considered donors to the campus for the service they provide. Groups falling under this category include the Arboretum Associates, Friends of the UCSC Library, Friends of the Farm and Garden, and the Women's Club, to name a few.

"UC Santa Cruz is very fortunate to have hundreds of friends and volunteers who generously give of their time, energy and resources that contribute to the educational experience on campus," says Liz Evanovich, community relations coordinator. "Our volunteers often mention the satisfaction that comes from being part of the life of a research university and the feeling of being personally enriched by their contributions."

Last year alone, UCSC students, staff and faculty contributed an estimated 1 million volunteer hours to schools and other nonprofits in Santa Cruz County. Nearly one-third of the 15,278 UCSC student body population volunteers or participates in unpaid internships throughout each school year.

"Internships are an integral part of many programs and majors on campus but not a requirement per se of all of them," says Evanovich. "The internships give students real-world experience in conjunction with their studies."

Membership in the Friends Groups is comprised of community members, staff, faculty and students.

Source: Liz Evanovich, Community Relations Coordinator, UC Santa Cruz, Santa Cruz, CA. Phone (831) 459-1325. E-mail: lize@ucsc.edu. Website: www.ucsc.edu

82 Virtual Food Drive Collects $9,000 ▬ ▬ ▬

For a fun, low-cost way to raise money, consider a virtual food drive similar to the one launched by the Food Bank of South Jersey (Pennsauken, NJ).

"'Let's Do Lunch' is a community-wide initiative that asks participating companies' employees to donate what they would normally spend on lunch one or more days that week to the Food Bank of South Jersey to help feed South Jersey's hungry," says Mario Partee, corporate partnerships manager. "Participants make selections from the menu. The total cost for the items they have chosen will be the amount the participant will be asked to donate. This allows participants to see the impact of their giving."

Partee explains how the program works:

- Food bank staff recruit local companies to participate in the program. The companies then encourage employees to participate.

- Food bank staff set up the virtual drive link for employees to access online. A printed food menu is available for persons who do not have Internet access.

- Persons log on or fill out paperwork, selecting what they would like for lunch. Choices determine dollar amount they would like to contribute. Donors can pay online by credit card or offline by check, cash or money order to a designated staff person.

- At week's end, the food bank staff tallies donations per participant. Some companies have a friendly competition to see which department raises the most funds.

The program's Thanksgiving/Holiday 2008 drive raised $9,000 from 122 participants. Partee says the fundraiser requires little investment other than set-up time, and adds that many people respond better to this method than traditional direct mail appeals.

Source: Mario Partee, Corporate Partnerships Manager, Food Bank of South Jersey, Pennsauken, NJ. Phone (856) 662-4884. E-mail: mpartee@foodbanksj.org

An interactive website pledge form helps people give to the online food drive for the Food Bank of South Jersey (Pennsauken, NJ).

Content not available in this edition

Article Designation Key: Donors ▬▬▬   Members ▬▬▬   Volunteers ▬▬▬

83   **Mini-websites Help Raise Funds for Nonprofit's Mission** ■ ■ ■

If your organization's membership and fundraising staff are stretched thin or you are simply looking for a way to engage members, consider sharing important duties with your supporters by creating a program that lets them take an active role in raising funds for your mission.

After years of donor-led fundraising events (e.g., birthday parties, weddings, special events, etc.) staff with the World Wildlife Fund (WWF) of Washington, DC, decided a change was needed, and launched Panda Pages in summer 2008.

Panda Pages is a section on WWF's website where persons create their own mini-websites to help raise money, raise awareness for the organization or a particular issue and connect with family and friends.

"The process of the fundraising events was cumbersome for donors and time-intensive for staff to manage," says David Glass, director, online marketing. "Our donors had to do much of the outreach, communication, fundraising and operations on their own. And, the entire effort was off-line, which made it challenging for a donor to gather and consolidate donations.

"It was time to give the donor much more control by putting the fundraising tools into the hands of our energetic and passionate supporters," he says.

Now by visiting the Panda Pages section (www.worldwildlife.org/mypanda) on WWF's website, supporters can customize a page in support of the organization's mission in about 10 minutes. The page can be customized to mark a special occasion, honor a friend or loved one, or simply highlight their passion for protecting endangered species.

The mini-websites allow supporters to:

✓ Send e-mails to friends and family asking them to visit the page.

✓ Raise money to help support WWF's conservation work.

✓ Connect with members who are passionate about wildlife conservation.

✓ Upload and share photos of favorite animals and nature places.

✓ Help protect endangered species and places around the world.

Since the program's launch, around 1,000 pages have been created.

Glass says supporters have two options when creating a page: public and private. A public page can be viewed or used by anyone who comes across the site, while only those who are specially invited may see a private page. Glass says near the holidays many families use the private pages to share information related to conservation and wildlife, conduct private fundraising, and share gift giving and donations online.

Source: David Glass, Director, Online Marketing, World Wildlife Fund, Washington, DC. Phone (202) 293-4800.
E-mail: David.glass@wwfus.org

Factors to Consider With User-based Fundraising Tool

A user-based fundraising tool like Panda Pages has several appealing benefits, says David Glass, director, online marketing, World Wildlife Fund (Washington, DC).

Those benefits include:

1. Donors and friends get a convenient, easy-to-use and efficient way to support their favorite cause.

2. The nonprofit gets an economical and efficient way to connect with many donors at a time for event-, theme- or topic-based fundraising.

Glass also shares two issues that are important to acknowledge with a new tool like this:

1. Putting more control in the hands of your organization's friends and donors means expecting and accepting that the messaging and language they use will vary and most likely be as on message as the language used by the organization to promote its own issues.

2. It's useful to build in training and awareness with a customer service team to help with any questions or concerns a donor may have.

Article Designation Key: Donors ▬▬▬   Members ▬▬▬   Volunteers ▬▬▬

84   Trusted Private Social Networks Provide Secure Option for Members ▬ ▬ ▬

Looking for new ways to create networking opportunities for your members? Consider a private social network, such as Affinity Circles (Mountain View, CA).

Established in 2002, Affinity Circles was a trusted and secure community created by Stanford students for both students and alumni who wanted to stay in contact with friends and colleagues. In 2003, the private social networking application was marketed to fellow alumni associations and organizations that could benefit from a member-based online community. Now more than 100 organizations use Affinity Circles platform for social networking.

Steve Loughlin, president and chief executive officer, explains the logistics of a private social network:

What are private social networks?

"A private social network is a secure online community that is accessible only to members of an alumni or professional organization that hosts it. Within this exclusive community, friends connect with friends, search for jobs, share expert knowledge, join professional groups, and share photos and blogs, all with the comfort of knowing their personal and professional communications are taking place within a secure setting they can trust."

How can a private online community help like-minded members?

"The trusted nature of a private community creates a unique environment for professional interactions. Because everyone is authenticated prior to entry, and all members share the same affinity, there is an increased sense of trust and rapport that encourages connections and an above-average willingness to help fellow community members. In addition,

members have the tools necessary to easily target others for insight, expertise, job leads or referrals and more. It's also easy to form groups or discussion topics based on interests, which in turn promotes knowledge sharing and builds stronger relationships within the community."

How do private social networks work?

"To gain entry, each member must be authenticated. Once inside, members are free to connect with one another, collaborate and share knowledge among themselves through events, forums, blog feeds, photo sharing. In addition, members can take advantage of inCircle Jobs, an online recruiting service that allows employers to target job postings directly to the private online communities of alumni and professional organizations."

For more information on private social networks, visit www.affinitycircles.com.

Source: Steve Loughlin, President and Chief Executive Officer, Affinity Circles, Mountain View, CA. Phone (650) 810-1500. E-mail: sloughlin@affinitycircles.com

---

Private Social Networking Also Benefits Organizations

Loughlin says a member organization that chooses to utilize private social networks will benefit in several ways:

- The network creates a clear and compelling value for the organization's brand. When members are able to connect, interact and share knowledge freely within the community, they associate that positive experience with the organization.

- Organizations can market more effectively to members by using online tools to reach members with personalized, relevant communications. Tapping into the personal profiles maintained by members also provides valuable insights on the community.

- Members have the tools necessary to help one another, which translates into real value for them — and for membership in the organization.

  - Increases member retention. Members find value in extending their physical relationships into the online environment. They can become more easily involved in a variety of programs, forums and activities — both online and off.

  - Members invite friends and colleagues to join the community. These free word-of-mouth referrals drive down new member acquisition costs.

Hosting a Private Social Network

Loughlin outlines the four steps involved in launching a private social network:

1. Sign a contractual agreement with Affinity Circles.

2. Provide graphics that brand the space for your community (e.g., a logo, your organization's name, etc.)

3. Upload your membership database. This will enable community members to identify people by location, profession and/or name from day one of the community's launch, unlike other networking sites.

4. The community is launched.

Content not available in this edition

| Article Designation Key: | Donors ▬▬▬ | Members ▬▬▬ | Volunteers ▬▬▬ |

85 Go Green: Use Website to Save Time, Resources, Environment ■ ■ ■

The need to save both financial resources and maximize time constantly challenges any volunteer manager. Here's an effort that is helping one nonprofit do both:

In a move to go green and save on paper, mailing and other costs related to producing printed pieces, Lee County Parks and Recreation (Fort Myers, FL) now posts most volunteer-related information online, says Kathy Cahill, volunteer services coordinator. The switch came as they sought to revamp their website to recruit, recognize and reward volunteers and — as mandated by the county — cut their paper budget by 50 percent.

By placing documents online, Cahill says they cut their paper budget by 80 percent.

The website now contains:

✓ Updated information on number of volunteers and volunteer hours.

✓ A list of volunteer opportunities.

✓ A way to sign up for the e-mail mailing list.

✓ Pictures of volunteers in action.

✓ Downloadable volunteer applications, handbooks, brochures and the incentive program catalog.

✓ The quarterly newsletter, "The Volunteer Times."

Moving the newsletter from a paper to an electronic format saved major costs and time by itself, Cahill says. Previously, 1,000 volunteers received a 12-page newsletter in the mail.

While Cahill still mails newsletters to a handful of volunteers (per their request), she says many volunteers prefer to access them online. The online resource is especially helpful to volunteers who are "snowbirds," in Florida just during the winter months.

Making the website a resource for volunteers also saves Cahill time. For example, when volunteers call, she can talk about their interests and direct them to the website for full position descriptions.

Source: Kathy Cahill, Volunteer Services Coordinator, Lee County Parks and Recreation, Terry Park, Fort Myers, FL. Phone (239) 432-2159. E-mail: kcahill@leegov.com

86 Small Organizations Can Level Playing Field With Online Giving ■

Like banking and shopping, charitable giving via the Internet is growing in popularity, and with good reason, says Katya Andresen, vice president, Network for Good (Bethesda, MD): "People love the convenience of online giving."

Although initial setup costs can seem overwhelming for some small nonprofits, Andresen says the giving method will quickly pay for itself. Not only will it help you reach a new, younger audience, the average online donation is more than $100, compared to the average offline donation of $27.

"It really levels the playing field," she says. "With online giving, you can compete with larger nonprofits."

When developing an online giving option, Andresen offers the following tips:

• **Communicate with social networks.** Send e-mails. Develop a reason for people to submit their e-mail address. For instance, offer weekly tips or a newsletter. However, make sure the information is interesting.

• **Develop effective messaging.** "It's not enough to have a 'donate now' button," Andresen say. "You need to put the proper messaging around that." She recommends answering four questions from the perspective of a potential donor: why me, what for, why now and who says?

• **Take proper cultivation steps**. "Don't treat online donors as 'walking wallets,'" Andresen says, reiterating the practice of thanking these and other donors three times more frequently than you ask them for a gift.

For more tips, she suggests visiting www.fundraising123. org. Part of Network for Good, this website offers free training opportunities and approximately 600 articles.

Source: Katya Andresen, Vice President of Marketing, Network for Good, Bethesda, MD. Website: www.networkforgood.org

---

Tips for Creating, Updating Websites

Here are three ideas to create or improve your organization's website for little cost:

1. Use a free resource specializing in website design and hosting (e.g., www. myspace.com or www.freeweb.com), which allows you to upload content and are easy to set up and maintain.

2. Talk to your organization's information technology department or webmaster about suggestions to update your website. Explain what you want to do and ask for help to get it done.

3. Turn to people who grew up online: high school and college students. Kathy Cahill, volunteer services coordinator, Lee County Parks and Recreation (Fort Myers, FL), was interviewing a University of Florida student and simply asked her if she knew Dreamweaver software (for website design). The student had been using the software for years to help out a friend's business website. She came on as an intern and taught the staff how to use the software.

87 Gain Insight With Member Polls ▪

Encouraging members to vote in online polls is an easy and cost-effective way to get their opinions on a wide variety of subjects.

The Alumni Association of Barry University (Miami Shores, FL) began using online polls in the summer of 2008. Alumni relations staff changes questions monthly, with roughly 500 to 1,000 members responding to each question.

Sean Kramer, assistant vice president, alumni relations, says he came up with the member poll idea as a way to make the alumni site more interactive. Currently, responses received by members are only used as anecdotal information and are not published. However, he says they will most likely publish poll responses in future issues of their e-news and alumni magazines.

Kramer shares a few examples of recent poll questions:

• What are your opinions of the new alumni association website?

• Have you attended an alumni association event in the past 6 months?

• How often do you utilize alumni association member benefits?

The university's information technology staff creates the online poll feature at no cost. The four-person alumni relations team comes up with the poll questions and IT staff updates the poll each month with the new question. Aside from including the poll feature on the alumni association website's home page, the polls are also mentioned in the university's e-news, which includes a link encouraging alumni to cast their vote.

When considering questions to include on an online poll, Kramer says, ask yourself:

• Is it information that will enhance our programs?

• Is it information that will benefit our members?

"Using these questions as a guideline should help organizations determine what questions to ask and when," says Kramer.

When designing a member poll feature, place it in a prominent section of your website so all of your members will notice it. If you are not sure whether to implement a new service or policy, a member poll is a great way to gain some insight into how your members will react to the change. You can also include questions about upcoming campaigns and special events to gauge member interest.

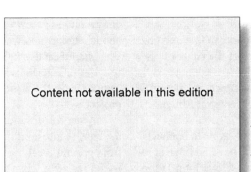

Content not available in this edition

Include a link to your member polls in your e-mail and written correspondence with members to provide them with another reminder to share their thoughts.

Source: Sean Kramer, Assistant Vice-President, Alumni Relations, Barry University, Miami Shores, FL. Phone (305) 899-4013. E-mail: SeKramer@mail.barry.edu

88 Offer Online Renewal, Giving ▪ ▪ ▪

Any steps you take to simplify the membership renewal process will help you maintain your member base.

The 6,500 members of The Walters Art Museum (Baltimore, MD) can conveniently renew memberships — and give them as gifts — online. Persons can also become members this way.

They can do so with a click of an interactive link at the museum's website (www.thewalters.org).

Why does the museum create these options? One simple reason: "Ease," says Elissa Winer, membership manager. "Computers and Internet commerce are a major part of modern-day life and the ability to offer anything over the Web is highly advantageous."

This fiscal year alone, 579 members opted to join or renew online with 18 members giving memberships as gifts. Winer says that with plans to continue upgrading the website, members will soon see even more interactive convenience down the road.

She offers these helpful tips to automate your website and attract members:

• Make membership options prominent on your website. Use highly visible links and buttons to offer easy enrollment. The use of uppercase letters also calls attention such as JOIN NOW or RENEW NOW.

• Make membership forms as easy and user-friendly as possible. If a member enters something incorrectly, be sure your system is automated to explain the need for correction with pop-up windows. Showing a sample of a correctly completed form also offers a visual example to those completing an enrollment and helps to eliminate errors.

• Automate the website by seeking out the best Web development company that provides the fit for your unique needs or ask a skilled staffer to automate the site. Evaluate the source based on budgetary issues, amount of traffic and message/information you wish to communicate.

Source: Elissa Winer, Membership Manager, The Walters Art Museum, Baltimore, MD. Phone (410) 547-9000. E-mail: ewiner@thewalters.org

89 Consider Webcam to Illustrate, Celebrate Building Process ▬ ▬ ▬

Do you have a major building project under way or on the horizon? Engage donors and potential donors in this exciting process to keep them involved and aware of the value of their support.

A webcam is helping capture the ongoing construction of the Bob and Shirley Hunter Welcome Center at Abilene Christian University (Abilene, TX).

"The webcam is a unique opportunity for us to connect donors to the project as well as those who have an interest in keeping up with developments on campus," says John Tyson, director of development. "It helps our friends and donors keep up with their investment and be reminded of how their funds are being used."

Before construction began, staff mounted a webcam to the university's campus bell tower and began shooting images of the construction site.

The webcam takes eight pictures per minute. Images are stored on a server and then uploaded to the university's website where visitors can click on a still image of the construction to view the live webcam (www.acu.edu/ aboutacu/map_acu/webcam.html).

Images on the website are refreshed every 60 seconds.

Kevin Watson, who oversees construction projects on campus, says the webcam will stay up for the duration of the project.

When construction is completed, he says, they can edit the images into a high-speed video that shows the building, from ground breaking to finish, in about three minutes — a useful resource when talking with donors and potential donors.

The 57,000-square-foot facility will be home to admissions, alumni relations, The ACU Foundation, the Center for Building Community and Career Center.

Sources: John Tyson, Director of Development; Kevin Watson, Administrative Services; Abilene Christian University, Abilene, TX. Phone (325) 674-2659 (Tyson) or (325) 674-2363 (Watson). E-mail: tysonj@acu.edu or watsonk@acu.edu

How a Webcam Works

The webcam capturing the construction of the Bob and Shirley Hunter Welcome Center at Abilene Christian University (ACU) of Abilene, TX is wired into the campus network, says Arthur Brant, director of networking services. The webcam works like a still camera, automatically taking and saving eight pictures a minute.

"The camera has Web server software that allows it to take and store pictures, which a second intermediate server can grab and store," says Brant. "The pictures on the university's website (www.acu.edu/aboutacu/map_acu/webcam.html), taken from the intermediate server, are refreshed every 60 seconds."

The webcam can be set to take as many as 30 pictures a second (full-motion video) to eight pictures a minute.

"We chose to go with a lower per-minute capture so as to not overwhelm our servers," he says. "We began taking pictures in December 2007 and are expecting 12 months of construction. At eight pictures a minute, we are taking 11,520 pictures in a given day and 4.2 million pictures by the end of the construction period. That many pictures can take up a lot of storage space."

Brant says they are storing all the pictures from the webcam so that they can create a stop-motion video encapturing the entire project, start to finish.

Webcams cost $800 to $1,000 depending on the quality of the images captured, says Brant. ACU's mid-quality camera cost about $1,000, plus the cost of a wide-view lens.

"For our purposes we wanted a middle-of-the-road camera," says Brant. "We aren't trying to do full-motion videos. We were more interested in giving people the online experience of a webcam."

Source: Arthur Brant, Director of Networking Services, Abilene Christian University, Abilene, TX. Phone (325) 674-2930. E-mail: branta@acu.edu

Article Designation Key: Donors ▬▬ Members ▬▬ Volunteers ▬▬

90 Craft an Online Presence and Interactive Approach ▪ ▪ ▪

The United Way of San Antonio and Bexar County (San Antonio, TX) offers a highly refined and effective interactive website, useful to both the volunteer and nonprofit organizations seeking to fill available positions.

The website (www.unitedwaysatx.org) offers a wealth of information for those seeking a volunteer opportunity. Here are three ways the website helps inform volunteers about the opportunities — ideas that could work for your organization's website:

- **Volunteer Solutions** — This section of the website currently lists 300 volunteer opportunities available in San Antonio and Bexar counties. Here, potential volunteers can search the database for the opportunity that best suits them. Volunteers can also save their areas of interest for faster future searches.

- **Ways of Caring Directory** — This online resource lists 200 agencies affiliated with the United Way of San Antonio and Bexar counties, offering a description of the agency, a list of typical jobs available at the agency, age requirements and other details useful to volunteers.

- **Special events** — Volunteer drives and details are listed on the website to draw attention to the volunteer opportunities available through the United Way. For example, the Days of Caring event listing explains its goal of partnering with local businesses to offer a weekend's worth of project-based volunteer opportunities.

Esther Cantú, director of volunteer programs and services, says listing all of these items and more at the organization's website draws more attention to the volunteer opportunities and makes the volunteer process simple and well defined.

Use the maximum potential of your website by listing specific opportunities, offering a volunteer search component, adding a resource database and emphasizing special volunteer events. This approach can save staff time and create an easy way for volunteers to access opportunities more readily. In turn, organizations in need of volunteers will fill those positions more quickly.

Source: Esther Cantú, Director of Volunteer Programs and Services, United Way of San Antonio and Bexar County, San Antonio, TX. Phone (210) 352-7000. E-mail: ECantu@unitedwaysatx.org

91 Link Blog Posts to Giving Page ▪ ▪ ▪

Keep people up to speed on your organization and its cause and boost fundraising efforts through a Web log or blog.

A blog "is a cost-effective way to stay in touch with supporters, spread our mission and beef up our online presence," says Robin Donovan, communications and outreach, Center for Respite Care (Cincinnati, OH).

"A blog is one tool nonprofits can use to keep supporters connected," Donovan says. "Supporters who feel that the day-to-day life of the organization is open to them are more likely to give. Plus, it is one more way to keep first-time volunteers, donors and friends engaged after their initial contact with us."

Blogs provide the perfect opportunity to promote special events, solicit in-kind donations, network and discuss issues important to your organization.

For example, a recent blog entry by Donovan explaining the need for helping the homeless in the winter included a direct link to the organization's online fundraising page.

Michael Foxworth, executive director, The Foothills Foundation/Foothill Presbyterian Hospital (Glendora, CA), also uses a blog as a key communications tool.

"Because the blog is, by nature, much more dynamic than the website and does not require extensive programming or HTML knowledge, nontechnical contributors can easily manage and post information to the blog," Foxworth says.

"There are many valuable blog hosting sites available for the beginner," he says. "Try it. If you can e-mail, you can blog."

Before you begin, Donovan recommends doing your research and being prepared to discuss the need of a blog. Additionally, she says, "learn to write in a style that works online and polish your writing to avoid excessive length. Post regularly, include photos and read related posts as much as you can. Also, read blogs about nonprofit blogging and communications."

Sources: Robin Donovan, Communications and Outreach, Center for Respite Care, Cincinnati, OH. Phone (513) 621-1868. E-mail: respitesupport@zoomtown.com. Blog: http://centerforrespitecare.wordpress.com Michael Foxworth, Executive Director, The Foothill Foundation/ Foothill Presbyterian Hospital, Glendora, CA. Phone (626) 857-3349. E-mail: mfoxworth@mail.cvhp.org. Blog: www.foothillfoundation.blogspot.com

92 Allow Members, Others to Shop Online ▪

Whether you seek to raise revenue, serve members, raise awareness or a combination of all those components, consider creating an online store to market your organization.

In June 2005, officials with the American Society of Radiologic Technologists (ASRT) of Albuquerque, NM, launched an online store as a matter of convenience, availability and cost savings, says Dina Hennessy, customer service director.

Hennessy suggests these steps to make your organization's online store more readily available to members and the public:

1. Identify and involve the appropriate stakeholders. This includes involving all the people who are a part of developing and implementing an online store (e.g., customer service department, the communications department and IT staff).

2. Decide the store's purpose.

3. Create a project plan including time line and key action items.

4. Determine whether the work will be done in-house or outsourced.

5. Define your customer. "For us this involved deciding that the store would service members and nonmembers," says Hennessy.

6. Research other online stores. "Visiting other sites allows you to pick and choose what you like so you can duplicate it and identify what you may have found difficult about another organization's site so you can steer away from that on your site."

7. Identify the product list.

8. Identify the features you'd like your store to have (e.g., shopping cart, FAQs [frequently asked questions] section, list of most popular items, etc.).

9. Build a test site.

10. Track the test results and create an issues list to identify high priority items.

11. Test, test and test some more.

12. Train staff.

13. Promote online store and provide customer education as needed.

14. Provide a mechanism for internal and external users to provide feedback.

15. Track and report results.

16. Identify changes for continuous improvement.

Hennessy says in fiscal year 2006-2007, the online store saved ASRT $18,000 in labor costs. The online store, which sells continuing education materials, generated around $156,000 with members' purchases totaling $151,367 and nonmembers' purchases totaling $4,425.

Source: Dina Hennessy, Customer Information Director, American Society of Radiologic Technologists, Albuquerque, NM. Phone (800) 444-2778, ext. 1318. E-mail: dhennessy@asrt.org

---

Online Store Sites

The American Society of Radiologic Technologists is one of numerous organizations enjoying the benefits online stores can bring (www.asrt.org/content/ASRTStore/productsresourceslanding.aspx).

For further inspiration, check out online stores for other member-based organizations:

- Pedaling History Bicycle Museum (www.pedalinghistory.com)
- Yellowstone Association (www.yellowstoneassociaton.org/store/)
- National Association for Gifted Children (www.nagc.org/acb/stores/1/index.aspx
- National Catholic Educational Association (www.ncea.org/store/)

---

93 Evaluate Your Site's Table of Contents ▪

Continually refine your website, as you do your other outreach materials, to capture your donors and potential donors interests.

Increasing numbers of nonprofit websites have several pages devoted to gifts or giving. When you click and arrive at the primary giving page, you find a table of contents that categorizes topics related to giving.

Put some thought into that index or table of contents to make it as easy as possible for website visitors to navigate your site. It's equally important that you prioritize what should be included in that listing.

Here is a sampling of headings from which you might choose in creating your gift section's table of contents:

❑ Alumni	❑ Corporate/Foundation Gifts
❑ Annual Gifts	❑ Annual Report
❑ Capital Campaign	❑ Case Statement
❑ Class Giving	❑ Gift Levels, Clubs
❑ Contact Us	❑ Ways to Become Involved
❑ Endowment	❑ Frequently Asked Questions
❑ Events	❑ Examples of Generosity
❑ Gift Opportunities	❑ How to Give
❑ Matching Gifts	❑ Naming Opportunities
❑ Planned Gifts	❑ Sponsorships
❑ Stewardship	❑ Strategic Plan

94

Online Social Networking
Benefits Users, Nonprofits ▬ ▬ ▬

Facebook. MySpace. LinkedIn. These and other online communities are all about networking and staying connected. Now some nonprofit organizations are joining in this trend, and finding it's a win-win situation.

MizzouNet is an online social community for alumni of the University of Missouri (Columbia, MO) and members of the Mizzou Alumni Association. Participants can keep in touch with friends, contact lost friends, network with alumni around the world, create and share photo albums, announce events and even search for jobs.

David Roloff, director of membership and marketing, calls MizzouNet a "professional version" of Facebook and "a great way to keep connected to the university and your peer group and network."

"We found that the more connected someone is as an alumni and the more they participate, the better it is for giving back to the university," says Roloff. "This does only good things for us. It keeps us connected."

Built by Affinity Circles (Mountain View, CA), MizzouNet is free to alumni and offered as a perk for students who are members of the alumni association. To access the network, persons visit the association's home page (www.mizzou.com) and click on the link to MizzouNet. From there, it is password protected.

MizzouNet launched in August 2006. The association created a basic profile with information it has for each of its potential users (e.g., name, graduation year, degree and a blind e-mail address, if available). From there users may register and further develop their profiles. Within the first year 7,000 persons registered profiles — well beyond the 3,000 goal, Roloff says. Currently, MizzouNet has 8,264 registered profiles, which is 3.7 percent overall participation. The classes of 2005 and 2006 have the most participation at 8.2 percent.

Roloff says while the growth of registered users has slowed, activity has not. To date, there have been 111,598 profile hits; 3,823 messages; 316 special interest groups formed; 241 event announcements; 89 blogs; and 63 forums.

When it debuted, university officials heavily promoted MizzouNet in e-mails to potential users, articles in the university magazine and electronic newsletter, and display ads in the magazine and on Facebook.

Roloff says maintaining the network is relatively easy. Since users control its content, maintenance is not an issue. A staff member validates registered profiles and answers minor technical questions. Affinity Circles staff handles the more complicated questions.

Creating an exclusive online network is easy, says Chuck Taylor, vice president of marketing and business development, Affinity Circles. Organizations provide his company with branding elements and membership data from which a marketing campaign is created. Setup is free, while Affinity Circles charges approximately $10,000 a year to host the community.

That's a small price to stay connected with potential donors, he says: "In a world where people are increasingly living their lives online, organizations must offer social networking tools for their members or face the threat of becoming irrelevant as their members connect with one another online in environments that do not feature the brand of the organization."

Sources: David Roloff, Director of Membership and Marketing, University of Missouri, Mizzou Alumni Association, Columbia, MO. Phone (573) 882-6611. E-mail: roloffd@missouri.edu. Chuck Taylor, Vice President of Marketing and Business Development, Affinity Circles, Inc., Mountain View, CA. Phone (650) 810-1500. E-mail: chuck@affinitycircles.com. Website: www.affinitycircles.com

Content not available in this edition

Four Ways Social Networking Boosts Fundraising Efforts

Chuck Taylor, vice president of marketing and business development, Affinity Circles, Inc. (Mountain View, CA), outlines ways social networking facilitates fundraising:

1. Engaging the member community on a much more regular basis than sporadic offline activities such as reunions and conferences.

2. Keeping member contact information current by synching the member profile data in the community with the organization's membership database.

3. Helping members share and receive valuable professional opportunities in a forum that reflects the organization's brand, standards and culture.

4. Collecting valuable social data on members (eg., hobbies and interests), the organization can use to market to them more effectively.

Article Designation Key: Donors ▭▭▭   Members ▬▬▬   Volunteers ▭▭▭

95 Boost End-of-year Giving With Online Wish List ▪ ▪ ▪

Wish lists are tried-and-true ways to generate targeted support at any time throughout the year but can prove especially beneficial as your organization nears its fiscal year end. As you approach the end of your fiscal year create and post an online wish list of items, projects and services for supporters to fund with their end-of-year gifts.

If you already have an online wish list, add some attention-getting items and get the word out about year-end opportunities through print and electronic communications.

Wish Lists May Be Basic 'Laundry Lists' or Highly Detailed Documents

Some organizations' wish lists include a simple checklist of needs (e.g., copy paper, postage stamps). Others go on to include a price estimate and brief description. Still others design highly detailed wish lists complete with photos, how the items will specifically benefit the nonprofit's mission and more.

The Berrien County Council for Children/The Children's Assessment Center (St. Joseph, MI) has a two-part wish list accessible by a direct link on its website's navigation bar (http://berrienchild.org/wish_list.html).

In addition to expected, less expensive wish-list items, such as printer cartridges and cleaning supplies, the nonprofit lists more creative ways to help, such as purchasing or partially funding an internal voicemail system ($3,000) or sponsoring brochure printing costs ($2,000).

Tia Miller, executive director, says since creating the online wish list in 2007, they have received a number of items, including office desks and children's supplies. She recommends being as specific as possible and including a price estimate to help guarantee you receive exactly what you need.

Another organization finding success with an online wish list is the Animal Medical Center (New York, NY). The wish list (shown in part at right) has brought in about $12,000 worth of gifts and goods in its first year, says Brandi Perrow, associate director of development.

The organization's wish list includes a photo, reason item is needed, cost and, if applicable, the amount raised toward the purchase of that item.

For example, a picture of a severely obese dog accompanies this text: "Fitness Maintenance for Fido. Some of our animal friends carry a little too much around the waist. Help the AMC obtain weight scales to monitor and manage obesity and diabetes. Needs: 1. Price Each: $1,200 ($300 raised)."

Offer Wished-for Items From Small to Large Price Ranges

When offering a wish list, Perrow says it is important to include items of varying costs to appeal to donors from all financial backgrounds.

What is the appeal of a wish list? "I think donors feel more connected when they can buy something on your list. They are fulfilling one of your wishes," Perrow says. Additionally, "Donors are getting very savvy, and they are

Content not available in this edition

concerned with where their money goes.... There is a comfort level with knowing exactly where their money is going and how it is being used."

Sources: Tia Miller, Executive Director, Berrien County Council for Children/The Children's Assessment Center, St. Joseph, MI. Phone (269) 556-9640. E-mail: tmiller@berrienchild.org Brandi Perrow, Associate Director of Development, The Animal Medical Center, New York, NY. Phone (212) 329-8662. E-mail: brandi.perrow@amcny.org. Website: www.amcny.org

96 Handling Online Renewal Challenges ▪

Moving to a new online member renewal system can be challenging for staff and members, says Kimberly Carbaugh, director of development and policy, Association of Nurses in AIDS Care (Akron, OH). The organization initiated such a system in November 2007.

To help staff adjust to the change, Carbaugh says ongoing training was held until staff familiarized themselves with the new process. Staff also took time to answer questions members had about the new website.

A majority of those questions involved members accessing the online renewal system. "Members have to log into the website, something they never had to do before," she says.

To keep members informed of the change, information was included in the quarterly newsletters, and weekly e-mails were sent including a statement about updating their information and a link to the website.

Lightning Source UK Ltd.
Milton Keynes UK
UKOW02f0028080813

214894UK00018B/331/P